Wanderings in Piccadilly, May Pall Mal

E. Beresford Chancellor

Alpha Editions

This edition published in 2024

ISBN 9789362993977

Design and Setting By
Alpha Editions
www.alphaedis.com
Email - info@alphaedis.com

As per information held with us this book is in Public Domain.
This book is a reproduction of an important historical work.
Alpha Editions uses the best technology to reproduce historical work
in the same manner it was first published to preserve its original nature.
Any marks or number seen are left intentionally to preserve.

Contents

PUBLISHERS' NOTE	- 1 -
PRESS OPINIONS.	- 2 -
CHAPTER I.	- 5 -
CHAPTER II.	- 26 -
CHAPTER III.	- 45 -
CHAPTER IV.	- 65 -
CHAPTER V.	- 85 -
FOOTNOTES:	- 101 -

PUBLISHERS' NOTE

Old London vanishes, another London takes its place; the interesting old spots associated with the leisurely life and refinement of the century that has gone, are being swept away one by one. In many ways we would welcome a return of those dear old days, with their appreciation of the *belles lettres* and the fine arts, and with all their oddities and quaint customs, but they have gone for ever. They played their part in the development of the national life: to us they are but memories.

We owe no small debt of gratitude, however, to those who—like the author—amidst all the changes that are taking place, have tried to keep alive for us with pen and pencil, a remembrance of a period so different from our own. Especially, perhaps, will many of our American cousins recognise this debt when in their migrations they try to hunt up places of interest connected with their English forbears.

Mr. Chancellor is most happy as he takes us round the old streets and houses, and gives—as it were—almost personal introductions to the quaint and interesting people who inhabited them. His pages are sentient with living[Pg vi] personages, and as we read we forget the years that have rolled away, while we enjoy the laugh and quip with the interesting old characters which are met with at every turn and corner.

To begin one's peregrinations at the corner of Bond Street and Piccadilly seems at first sight a little arbitrary, but one soon realises that in starting from "Stewart's," and keeping within a half-mile radius of this centre, one is really covering by far the most interesting portion of the West End; while the old shop, which—during more than two centuries—has given its name to this corner of Bond Street, and which, as Mr. Chancellor declares, is to Americans one of the best known spots in Europe, is in itself a most interesting link with the past and present.

The Author, and the Publishers, acknowledge with thanks their indebtedness to Edward Gardner, Esq., for kind permission to reproduce six views of Old London from his unique Collection of Drawings and Prints.

PRESS OPINIONS.

"A good little book for pilgrims, 'more especially,' as it states, 'those from America,' who wish to recognise the multitude of distinguished ghosts who crowd the district dealt with."—*Graphic.*

"Always readable and interesting. The chief attraction of the book, which, by the way, is charmingly 'got up,' is to be found in the twenty plate illustrations of Old London streets and houses. Four are successful reproductions in colour."—*Antiquarian.*

"In this pretty little book ... these notes on the heart of the West End are made to gyrate round Stewart's Tea Rooms at the corner of Bond Street, called 'Stewart's Corner.' The publisher seems to have felt that to assume this shop to be the hub of the best part of London is sufficiently remarkable to require explanation, so he writes:—'To begin one's peregrinations at the corner of Bond Street and Piccadilly seems at first sight a little arbitrary, but one soon realizes that in starting from "Stewart's" and keeping within a half-mile radius of this centre, one is really covering by far the most interesting portion of the West End.' The plates, which are mostly reproductions of old prints, are singularly interesting (especially the coloured ones), and are themselves worth the price of the book."—*Athenæum.*

"Mr. Chancellor guides the reader round the old streets and houses, introducing him personally, as it were, to the quaint and interesting people who inhabited them."—*The Queen.*

"A little book gathering up in a quite popular way some of the associations of the district, with many illustrations of it as it appeared in the past."—*"Times" Literary Supplement.*

"The author of 'The Squares of London' has in a high degree the faculties of selection and concentration, and in his hundred and fifty pages he has been able to tell us so much and to tell it so well."—*Illustrated Sporting and Dramatic News.*

"There is no lack of interest, past and present, in the district about which our author discourses. Piccadilly is notorious for its 'ghosts'; and St. James's Street, Park Lane, Grosvenor Square, Pall Mall, Albemarle Street, to name a few places at random, have an abundant population of the same kind. This little volume, which is judiciously illustrated, makes good reading."—*The Spectator.*

"A pretty little book this, with charming illustrations of the West End in days of old, four of them in colour. The pages are rich in brief anecdote, as well as topographical details of interest."—*The Lady's Pictorial.*

"It is just the book for the Londoner who is always interested in the old spots that are being swept away one by one; and the novice who knows nothing of the subject will be fascinated by these pictures of former days."—*Methodist Times.*

"Those who are interested in this class of literature will find Mr. Chancellor's book interesting, all the more so if they have some acquaintance with the English literature of the last two centuries. The area covered is large, but there is no lack of interest, past and present, in our author's discoursings about it. The volume is judiciously illustrated."—*Catholic Times.*

"Pictures of St. James's Street in George the Third's reign, the palace at the foot in the days of the Stuarts, Carlton House during the Regency, together with various old inns, mansions, and other vanished buildings, combine to make an illustrated gallery of a departed era."—*The Bookseller.*

"Famous streets, famous buildings, famous men. Mr. Chancellor catalogues them in an agreeable literary form, with plenty of notes and incidents and historic origins."—*The Globe.*

"Mr. Chancellor's small volume is among the best. It has a real literary flavour, and is full of reminiscences of times long past. The twenty illustrations of old London (four of them in colour) are particularly well chosen."—*Publishers' Circular.*

"A compact memorial volume like this is of special value. We are conducted round the fine old streets and famous houses, and are given almost personal introductions to the famous and quaint folk who inhabited them."—*Christian Commonwealth.*

"In hunting up places of interest connected with our forbears, the author has endeavoured, and successfully, to keep alive for us a remembrance of a past period."—*Broad Arrow.*

"A pleasant sketch describing the West End of London in the eighteenth and the early part of the nineteenth century, drawing a vivid picture of life in that part of London at that time, and giving details concerning many famous buildings."—*Record.*

"This charming little work must needs be invaluable to all lovers of London, among whom the author reckons our American cousins, for whose more especial benefit he has given a map of the district in two parts, one representing the Eastern and the other the Western limits of his rambles."—*Western Morning News.*

"Mr. Chancellor recalls many historical facts about these old streets and houses, re-peopling them with English men and women of long ago, telling anecdotes and gossiping in pleasantest manner."—*Yorkshire Daily Post.*

"There is much to be learned from these pages how these parts of London came to be built, and why the streets bear various strange names, of which Maddox is one."—*Nottingham Guardian.*

"The author of 'The Squares of London' has undoubtedly done a great deal to keep alive for us, with a ready and able pen, memories of the old London which are tending to become less and less distinct with the march of time and the rush of new ideas."—*Huddersfield Examiner.*

"The book is full of delightful gossip regarding the clubs, theatres, and great houses of past and present times."—*The Northern Whig.*

"A capital and interesting book of its kind, full of pleasant reminiscences of the days of the leisurely life and refinement of the century that has gone."—*Manchester Evening News.*

"The volume is well illustrated, and the reproductions from old prints and drawings of mansions which have altogether disappeared—as, for instance, Northumberland House, with its famous lion—are particularly interesting."—*Glasgow Herald.*

"This admirable book is packed full of historical and biographical information, retailed in the pleasantest possible manner."—*Liverpool Daily Courier.*

"Mr. Chancellor is an excellent cicerone in describing for us the old streets and houses and the quaint people who inhabited them."—*Yorkshire Herald.*

"With this little book in his pocket (where it will hardly reveal itself), or on his table, the visitor to London can add greatly to his enjoyment."—*Aberdeen Journal.*

"A delightful little guide to the localities mentioned."—*Aberdeen Free Press.*

"With this book in the coat pocket—to glance at in convenient corners—one could spend some pleasant hours."—*Bolton Journal.*

CHAPTER I.

PICCADILLY.

"By night or by day, whether noisy or stilly,
Whatever my mood is—I love Piccadilly."
LOCKER-LAMPSON.

Dr. Johnson in one of his rhetorical flights said that Charing Cross was practically the centre of the universe. "I think," he observed to Boswell, on a celebrated occasion, "the full tide of human existence is at Charing Cross." Theodore Hook, on the other hand, considered that that small area in St. James's, bounded by Piccadilly and Pall Mall, St. James's Street and Waterloo Place, was the acme of fashion, and contained within itself all that was best worth cultivating in the Metropolis.

Like all generalizations, neither of these dicta will bear the test of logical analysis. Hook's favourite quarter has undergone many a change, and its present-day equivalent is more likely to be found in that larger area known to all the world as Mayfair. Similarly, although much of the tide of human existence still flows past the spot where Queen Eleanor's body rested for the last time, on its way to the Abbey, that tide flows as fully and with as much noisy vehemence past half a hundred other crowded spots in London. It is probable, however, that at no one point does it surge and rage (to carry on the metaphor), with greater force than at the spot where Piccadilly and Bond Street join. At this spot stands "Stewart's"—famed all the world over. I say "Stewart's," as I should say in Venice, "Florian's," or in New York, "Delmonico's"; for there are certain famous establishments in all great cities which require no more specific designation.

Who is there, indeed, that knows not Stewart's? It has been presiding over this corner for the last two hundred years and more. It must be the oldest baker's and confectioner's business in London, beside which even such ancient houses as "Birch's" or "Gunter's" are comparatively modern. To-day it bears upon its rebuilt front, the date of its establishment—1688, and the massive foundations and old brickwork, which were brought to light during the recent rebuilding, fully support the theory that this was one of the original buildings erected by Sir Thomas Bond on the site of Clarendon House, when he laid out the street which bears his name.

Let us take this shop, as characteristic of many others, and try to recall what it may have witnessed in the lapse of years. In its early days it was, no doubt, too much occupied with its own affairs to take much note of great personages or historic events; but after it had settled down, so to speak, and had become, as it did, the purveyor of the staff of life to the Coffee-houses that had sprung up around it, it may be supposed to have given an eye, now and then, to the interesting men and beautiful women who passed by, or who made it a rendezvous while some of them waited for those who were spending or making fortunes in the gambling hells of St. James's Street hard by.

Stewart's Corner
Old Bond S▢ & Piccadilly
REBVILT 1907.

The Augustan age is here! Can that little shrivelled body limping along, having just come from its lodging in Berkeley Street, contain the great mind of Alexander Pope? Surely 'tis he, having but this moment penned a letter to Martha Blount, or put the finishing touches to his "Farewell to London." He is probably on his way to visit my lord Burlington, whose home (the precursor of the later mansion built by his great grandson, and now known by the massive buildings of the modern Burlington House), is close by. Horace Walpole tells us that when asked why he built his mansion so far *out of town*, the first Earl replied, "Because he was determined to have no building beyond him!" *Credite posteri!* but he meant, and should have added, "to the north," which is, in itself, wonderful enough for us to realize now, for Clarendon House and Berkeley House were already in existence to the west. Could it have been Pope, who asked the question? It seems likely, for we remember the anecdote of the irate gentleman who being in the poet's company and required to give a definition of "a point of interrogation," replied "that it was a little crooked thing that asked questions!"

And then that fine looking man in the full bottomed wig, can that be Mr. Addison of the *Spectator*, fresh from his lodgings in the Haymarket hard by, and still glowing in the reflected glory of "The Campaign?" None other. And lo! here is the handsome face of his hero, who "taught the doubtful battle where to rage," as he hobbles along (he will soon be off to Bath to try and cure his gout)—fit indeed, *monstrari digito*, for other things besides his military glory. He will not turn in at Stewart's we may be sure, for if the "tears of dotage" have not yet begun to flow, at least he is learning to save his money.

Here, too, comes jolly Dick Steele; he has just been into a coffee house to pen a line of excuse to his "dearest Prue," in Kensington Square, and is on his way to a jollification with some of his boon companions; forgetful of his "Apology," and hardly living up to the ethics of his "Christian Hero." Still with all his faults, a pleasanter figure to meet than that dark-faced, dissatisfied-looking man in clerical attire. That is the redoubtable Dean Swift himself, one of the great geniuses, not only of his own day, but of all time. He knows this part of the town as well as he knows all the turns and twists of contemporary politics; and has probably come from his rooms in Ryder Street almost opposite. Wherever he is he will be penning that famous "Journal to Stella," or plotting and planning with the heads of the Opposition—and there is no clearer or more potent brain among them. If he goes into the St. James' Coffee House, or White's Chocolate House, "the most fashionable hell in London," or trudges further east to Willis's, in Bow Street, be sure there will be plenty to note his strange manner and call him "the mad parson!" Perchance he may be taking the air to prepare himself for that particular dinner with my Lord Abercorn when there smoked upon the board the "fine fat haunch of venison, that smelt rarely on one side," which he mentions, with such gusto, in his journal; or perhaps he is setting out on one of his long rambles to Chelsea to dine with the Dean of Carlisle, or to sup with Lord Mountjoy at Kensington Gravel Pits.

An observant traveller who visited London about this period, remarks that "Most of the streets are wonderfully well lighted, for in front of each house hangs a lantern or a large globe of glass, inside of which is placed a lamp which burns all night." The light which hung before "Stewart's" must have illuminated the face of many a "toast," many a "Macaroni," as they came up Bond Street, and sometimes that of one of those terrible "mohocks." My Lord Mohun, not yet dreaming of his sanguinary and fatal encounter with his grace of Hamilton, but sufficiently notorious for that mysterious affair when Mountfort the player fell mortally wounded near his lodging in Norfolk Street; the eccentric Duke of Wharton, who once sent a bear to his tutor as an appropriate concomitant to his "bearish conduct"; who, marrying at sixteen, became a sort of Jacobite hero, and showed by some of his writings in "The True Briton," what gifts he had squandered by a riotous life; and who finally ended his career in a Bernardine Convent, "the scorn and wonder of our days," as Pope writes, "a sad outcast of each church and state." Hervey, the "Sporus" of the same bitter pen, having dragged himself for a space from the Court, of which he was so characteristic an ornament, and from the company of the Princess who secretly loved him. Perhaps he will to-morrow fight, behind Arlington House, hard by, with Pulteney, who called him "a thing below contempt." That slip of the foot at the critical moment saved the "thin-spun life," and like so many protagonists in such encounters, the whilom enemies embrace, with more fervour on Pulteney's part than on that of "My Lord" who but bows in silence and withdraws.

And then what a galaxy of beauty reflects the light from that "lantern or large globe of glass!" Here is Lady Mary Wortley Montagu, not very much affected by the virulent lines of the "wicked wasp of Twickenham"; the lovely Molly Lepel, who married Lord Hervey, and whom Lady Suffolk loved so much; Mary Bellenden, afterwards Mrs. Campbell, another of those maids of honour whom Gay and Prior sung, and Swift and Arbuthnot undertook to prove the best wives, although we remember that the coachman at Leicester House solemnly forbade his son ever to think of any of them in so tender a way! Here, too, is Lady Mary Coke, who was used to almost regard herself as a royal widow, on the death of Edward Duke of York—for which "mealy faced boy" she had a "*tendre*"; the Duchess of Queensberry, Prior's "Kitty ever fair," whom Walpole thought looked "(by twilight) like a young beauty of an old-fashioned century," and who died in Savile Row, in 1777, "of a surfeit of cherries."

The list might be indefinitely extended, but "*Anni labuntur*" and other centuries are hurrying us along, bringing new faces in their train; George Selwyn with his witty talk and mania for executions; he is off now, probably to see John Rann, or "Sixteen-stringed Jack," as he was called, strung up at

Tyburn tree—my Lord Pembroke accompanies him, and the cronies chancing to meet a lot of young chimney sweeps who beg for money, Selwyn suddenly addresses them solemnly with the words "I have often heard of the sovereignty of the people. I suppose your highnesses are in Court mourning;" Charles James Fox, the most eminent of those "sons of faro," who having lost his last penny and consoled himself by reading Homer in the small hours, is thinking of a "passover" to the Continent, which, as Selwyn says, will *not* be relished by the Jews; Lord March may also be seen, the wicked "old Q" of many a notorious story; and Hare—"the hare with many friends," as his acquaintances nick-named him; and then the dandies of a later day; Alvanley, who succeeded Selwyn as a wit and almost rivalled Brummell as a dandy; "Ball" Hughes and "Teapot" Crawfurd; Lord Yarmouth and Prince Esterhazy; Jack Lee, and the great Brummell himself, who has cut the Regent and is thinking of bringing the old king into fashion!

These, and how many others, have not passed by that corner in Piccadilly where Stewart's stands; they are but the ghosts of the beauties and exquisites of a bygone day that loiter there—for in this strenuous age no one dawdles—all is hurry and confusion, and the idle stroller, other than Thespian, is almost a thing of the past. Let us for the moment try to imitate our forbears and "take a walk down Piccadilly."

What changes have not taken place in this street of streets! It was known by the quaint name it still bears as early as 1633, for Gerarde in his famous Herbal, mentions "the wild bu-glosse," that "grows about the drie ditch-bankes about Pickadilla." This is not the place to go into the mysteries of nomenclature, and many have been the theories as to the origin of the name; but that is probably the correct solution which traces it to the ruffs called Pickadils, worn by the gallants of James's and Charles's time. Blount in his "Glossography" (1656) thus speaks of the matter: "A Pickadil is that round hem, or the several divisions set together about the skirt of a garment or other thing; also a kind of stiff collar, made in fashion of a band. Hence, perhaps, the famous ordinary near St. James's, called Pickadilly, took denomination, because it was then the utmost, or skirt house of the suburbs, that way."

Thus Blount, and I think we may leave it at that. We shall return later on to the "famous ordinary," which was known as Pickadilla Hall, and was situated at the north-east corner of the Haymarket: now we are on our way west, like the wise men of old.[1]

ALBEMARLE STREET.

The first tributary street we come to is Albemarle Street, formed, at the same time as Bond Street, about 1684, by Sir Thomas Bond, on the site of

Clarendon House, which the great Lord Clarendon built from the designs of Pratt, according to Evelyn, on ground which had been granted him by Charles II., in 1664. The Diarist had "never seen a nobler pile," and he had every opportunity for criticising it thoroughly as, on one occasion, the Chancellor himself showed him all over it; and the extant views of it fully confirm Evelyn's enthusiasm. The populace, however, saw in the great place the results of bribery and corruption, and Dunkirk House, Holland House, and Tangier House, were titles freely applied to it. On Clarendon's death, the house was sold (1675) to the second duke of Albemarle (the son of the great Monk) for £26,000 (it had cost £40,000 originally). In consequence of extravagance in all sorts of ways, however, its new owner was not long able to keep it, and he in turn sold it, it is said, for £20,000, to Sir Thomas Bond, who pulled it down and built Albemarle Street (then called Albemarle Buildings), and Bond Street on its site. Evelyn, on September 18th, 1683, notes that he "walked to survey the sad demolition of Clarendon House, that costly and only sumptuous palace of the late Lord Chancellor Hyde," "where," he adds, "I have often been so cheerful with him and sometimes so sad."

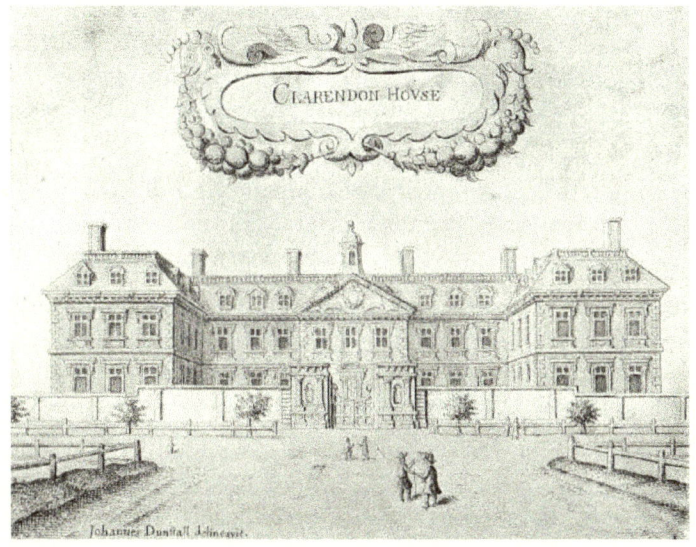

CLARENDON HOVSE
(*From a print of the period.*)

Albemarle Street, "of excellent new buildings, inhabited by persons of quality," as the New View of London (1708) describes it, has had some interesting inhabitants. Here, in 1712, Sir William Wyndham and his family escaped in their night clothes from the fire that destroyed his house, for which he had given £6,000, as he told Swift, when many rare pictures and other valuables were destroyed; here, in Lord Grantham's house, lived for a time the Prince of Wales, afterwards George II., until he moved to Leicester House. Bishop Berkeley was lodging at Mr. Fox's (an apothecary's) in this street, from 1724 to 1726, as he records in his "Literary Relics," and Sir Richard Mead, who formed that fine collection of drawings subsequently added to the Royal Collection, resided here in 1720.

Many years later the Duc de Nivernois was lodging in the street, and here received on one occasion Gibbon "more as a man of letters than as a man of fashion," much to the latter's chagrin. Lord Bute, another minister who became, as Clarendon had done, an object of popular hatred, was living here in 1764; and there is a story told by Lord Malmesbury, that when a Mr. Calvert asked in the House of Commons "Where is Athens? What is become of Lacedæmon?" some member of the Opposition called out that "they had gone to Albemarle Street."

It is obviously possible to do little more than mention the names of some of the other distinguished residents in Albemarle Street. Here lived Zoffany, the painter, who executed, about this period, a portrait of Wilkes, "looking—no, squinting—at his daughter," as Walpole records: Robert Adam, the architect of so many fine dwellings, died here, in 1792, and his brother James two years later, at No. 13; Charles James Fox was living here when Rogers first knew him; Sir James Mackintosh was at No. 26, on his return from India in 1811, and "Leonidas" Glover, died in a house here, in 1785.

Albemarle Street has been noted for its hotels. Here was Dorant's, where Byron stayed, when he was publishing his "Hours of Idleness"; and the famous Grillion's, where Louis XVIII. in exile held his Court.

The name of Byron brings us appropriately enough to No. 50, Albemarle Street—for here the great publishing firm of Murray, so closely connected with his name, has been settled since John Murray removed hither from Fleet Street, in 1812.

The columnar façade of the Royal Institution, the work of Vulliamy, forms a curiously solemn note in Albemarle Street, but its importance as a great scientific centre more than justifies its severe, almost melancholy, appearance.

DOVER STREET.

Dover Street, to which we come a few steps further west, was built about 1686, and was named after Henry Jermyn, Lord Dover. He lived in a house which was subsequently advertised for sale in the "Daily Journal" for January, 1727. It would appear that after his death his widow had been residing here, for the notice indicates that the cause of the sale was that lady's decease. Mention is particularly made of a beautiful staircase painted by Laguerre, as well as "all manner of conveniences for a great family." The house was on the east side, and not far from it, Evelyn came to dwell in 1699, having taken the lease of a residence on the same side of the street. That mad Duke of Wharton whom I have already mentioned, also lived in Dover Street, "in a most sumptuous building, finely finished and furnished"; so did the great Robert Harley, Earl of Oxford, as well as his son, the second Earl, who married the heiress of the Duke of Newcastle. Pope used to stay here as a guest at this time; and as Arbuthnot was also living in the same street these two friends would often, we are to suppose, discuss that "half pint of claret" which the latter humorously told Pope, he could still afford. Another of this coterie, Bolingbroke, was wont to lodge at "Mr. Chetwynd's," as Gay informs Swift, probably with a view to a philosophic, albeit, a merry meeting there. Sir William Wyndham was also a former resident; so was Miss Reynolds, the sister of Sir Joshua, whom Johnson used to visit; Lord King, the biographer of Locke; Archdeacon Coxe, who wrote ponderous tomes about Sir Robert Walpole and the House of Austria, and Nash, the architect, who built the more imposing portion of Regent Street.

But the two most interesting houses were (for one has disappeared, and its site is covered by a mushroom block of red brick flats, and although the other still remains, it is empty and will probably soon go the way of all old buildings) Ashburnham House and Ely House.

The former, with its gateway and lodge designed by Robert Adam in 1773, was the town house of the Earls of Ashburnham, but others beside that family occasionally inhabited it, and for a time it was the Russian Embassy; Prince Lieven being the first ambassador residing here, and Pozzo di Borgo the last.

Ely House, designed by Sir Robert Taylor, has been, since 1772, the town residence of the Bishops of Ely, and was conveyed to that See in exchange for Ely Place, Holborn.

Dover Street has always been rather famous for its hotels, and in this respect at least, its reputation is well sustained. Le Telier's was one of the older ones, and is notable as being the house to which the Literary Club moved from Sackville Street, before going into St. James's Street.

THE WHITE HORSE CELLAR.

Just before we reach Berkeley Street, we come to Hatchett's Restaurant, the old "White Horse Cellar," so named from the emblem in the crest of the House of Hanover. The old original "White Horse Cellar," whence in the good old days the coaches left on their way to the west, stood nearly opposite, close to Arlington Street. As may be seen from old sporting prints, the outside of the original house was covered on particular occasions with oil lights of various colours—lights which many a jaded traveller must have seen with pleasure, and many a fresh one left with regret. One of these occasions was the King's birthday, when the coachmen and guards donned new scarlet liveries, and even the coaches were touched up. Sir Vincent Cotton, Capt. Probyn, Lord Worcester and Sir Thomas Jones were among the amateur whips who frequently handled the ribbons and tooled their coaches down the intricacies of Piccadilly; and we can quite believe Hazlitt when he says that "the finest sight in the metropolis is the setting off of the mail coaches from Piccadilly."

THE WHITE HORSE CELLAR—HATCHETT'S RESTAURANT—
PICCADILLY
(From a Drawing by George Cruikshank.)

How many of us would not have given a good round sum to have seen Mr. Pickwick laboriously climb on to the top of the vehicle which was to carry him to Bath, or Sam Weller's surprise when he observed the name of "Pickwick" painted on the coach door; or "the young man of the name of Guppy," meeting Esther Summerson here on her arrival in London one foggy afternoon in November; or Jerry Hawthorn "fairly knocked up by all the excitement, getting into the coach"—being one of six inside, "what time his friends shake him by the hand, whilst the Jews hang round with oranges, knives and sealing wax, whilst the guard is closing the door." All we can do is to rehabilitate the scene of the former from Dickens's pen; and to imagine ourselves watching the latter in Cruickshank's drawing.

Another hostelry from which coaches departed on their long journeys was the "Gloucester Coffee House," kept by one Dale, which stood where the Berkeley Hotel, formerly known as the St. James's Hotel, is now; and "The Green Man and Still" was yet another house of call for the coaches that went westward.

BERKELEY STREET.

Berkeley Street, formerly known as Berkeley Row, boasts one or two interesting residents in the past. Here Cosway dwelt, and it was here that he first attracted the notice of the Prince of Wales, whose portrait he "drew in little" so often and so successfully. In the same house, too, had previously lived Shackleton, the portrait painter; and it was to a residence here that Mr. Chaworth was carried after his duel with Lord Byron (the great uncle of *the* Lord Byron), which took place at the "Star and Garter," in Pall Mall, over a dispute as to the best way of preserving game. Lord Byron, the survivor, underwent his trial in Westminster Hall, but was acquitted, and a certain French traveller, M. Grosley, who was present at the trial, saw his lordship a few days later taking part in the debate on the Regency Bill, as if nothing had happened.

DEVONSHIRE HOUSE.

The long front of Devonshire House, with its fine gates, which were originally at the Duke's place at Chiswick, now faces us. It was erected from the designs of Kent, for the third Duke of Devonshire, two years after Berkeley House had been burnt down (in 1733). Its beautiful grounds are only divided from those of Lansdowne House by Lansdowne Passage, a short cut, sunk below the ground level, from Curzon Street to Hay Hill. There are iron bars at each end of this passage, and probably few people know why they were placed there. As a matter of fact, they were put up in consequence of a mounted highwayman in the eighteenth century, after having got away from Piccadilly with some booty, riding his horse through this passage and up the steps at the end. Thomas Grenville is the authority for this anecdote, and the robber was seen galloping past his residence in Bolton Street.

THE GLOUCESTER COFFEE HOUSE, PICCADILLY.

Devonshire House is one of the great houses of London, and is full of Art treasures, a list of which alone would fill a volume; particularly remarkable is the collection of drawings by the old masters, which includes the original "Liber Veritatis" of Claude de Lorraine; and a superb collection of engravings by Marc Antonio—to mention but these. In the library is the great Kemble collection of old plays, including the first four folios of Shakespeare's works, &c., which the sixth Duke bought for £2,000. What are they not worth now?

The portico replaced, in 1840, the old entrance which was by a flight of steps on each side; and among the other improvements made by the sixth Duke was the addition of a fine marble staircase up which all the great ones of several generations have passed, from the days when the beautiful Duchess welcomed Fox here, and the Prince Regent, "surrounded by the first Whig families in the country," stood to see the apotheosis of the "man of the people" after the Westminster election, to days within memory, when Dickens and his friends acted here for charity.

STRATTON STREET.

Beyond Devonshire House is Stratton Street, which is, of course, named after Lord Berkeley, the hero of Stratton fight. Although there have been one or two interesting people living in this street in the past, such as Campbell, the poet, who was here in 1802; James Douglas, the author of "Nenia Britannica"; and Lord Lynedoch, who was second in command in the Peninsula, the chief interest attaching to it is the fact that at No. 1, which belonged to Coutts, the banker, and looks on to Piccadilly, lived for many years, until her death quite recently, the venerable Baroness Burdett-Coutts. The house next door, No. 80, Piccadilly, with its old-fashioned front and painted glass windows to the ground floor rooms, was for many years the residence of her father, Sir Francis Burdett, and it was from here that, in 1810, he was taken to the Tower. For two days he successfully barricaded himself in the house, but entrance being eventually forced, he was found, somewhat theatrically, teaching one of his children Magna Charta. The riots consequent on this incarceration are mentioned at length in many of the letters and diaries of the period; and the soldiers, for their share in suppressing them, were termed "Piccadilly Butchers."

The house next door (No. 81) stands on the site of the celebrated Watier's Club, established in 1807. Watier had been cook to the Prince of Wales, and although his gastronomic skill was unquestionable, and although Brummell was the presiding genius (or, was it because of that fact?), the club, which had been the ruin of many a member, only existed for about 12 years, according to Gronow, whose well-known story of its origin, may be repeated here:—

"Upon one occasion some gentlemen of both White's and Brookes's had the honour to dine with the Prince Regent, and, during the conversation, the Prince inquired what sort of dinner they got at their clubs, upon which Sir Thomas Stepney, one of the guests, observed, 'that their dinners were always the same, the eternal joints or beefsteaks, the boiled fowl with oyster sauce, and an apple-tart; this is what we have at our clubs, and very monotonous fare it is.' The Prince, without further remark, rang the bell for his cook, Watier, and in the presence of those who dined at the Royal table, asked him whether he would take a house and organize a dinner-club. Watier assented, and named Madison, the Prince's page, manager, and Labourie, from the Royal kitchen, the cook."

It was here that once, on Brummell's calling with a tragic air to a waiter to bring a pistol, for he had been losing heavily, one of the members, Bob Leigh, who proved to be mad, said, "Mr. Brummell, if you really wish to put an end to your existence, I am extremely happy to offer you the means," at the same time producing two loaded pistols from his pockets and laying them on the table; and here, too, Jack Bouverie threw his bowl of counters at the head of Raikes who had been making some ill-timed jests at his losses.

BOLTON STREET.

Bolton Street here joins Piccadilly. Formed in 1699, it was described by Hatton, a few years later, as "the most westerly street in London, between the road to Knightsbridge, south, and the Fields, north." Here both Martha and Theresa Blount once lived, and were called the "Young Ladies in

Bolton Street" by their admirer, Pope. The poet not only visited them here, but was also occasionally the guest of the eccentric Earl of Peterborough, who lived in the same street for fourteen years, from 1710. George Grenville, also resided in Bolton Street, as did another politician, Lord Melbourne; and at least three notable ladies are connected with this vicinity, Fanny Burney (Madame D'Arblay), who came to live in the street in 1818, shortly after the death of General D'Arblay, and was visited by Scott and Rogers and many another fashionable and literary notabilities; Mrs. Delany, who lived in the adjoining Bolton Row in 1753; and Mrs. Vesey, whose evening parties probably kept the quieter denizens of the street awake o'nights.

If, as is sometimes reported, Prince Charles Edward really did pay a visit to London in 1760, and was present at the Coronation, then he set out for the Abbey from a house in Bolton Street, for here he is said to have lodged, without even "the semblance of a kingly crown" about his brows.

BATH HOUSE.

When Horace Walpole, who loved not his father's old enemy, Lord Bath, wrote on one occasion that "the grass grows just before my Lord Bath's door, whom nobody will visit," he indicated the large house still known as Bath House which occupies much of the western side of Bolton Street, and which was originally built by William Pulteney, Earl of Bath, on whom so many bitter epigrams were written, and whose parsimony was so notorious. As an example of the former, I may remind the reader of those lines "written on the Earl of Bath's door in Piccadilly," by Sir Charles Hanbury Williams, which run thus:

"Here dead to fame lives patriot Will,

His grave a lordly seat,

His title proves his epitaph,

His robes his winding sheet."

As a proof of the latter, is extant the story that having visited Holkham, and forgetting to tip the servants, a pang of conscience spurred his lordship to send back a horseman six miles, *with half a crown*. An even better illustration of his ostentation and meanness combined is preserved by George Colman, who relates that when driving through the lodge gates of his country house, word would be given to halt; the outriders repeated the order, the coachman pulled up his four horses, and from the becoronetted carriage, William Pulteney, Earl of Bath, Viscount Pulteney, of Evington,

Baron of Hedon, P.C., F.R.S., etc., etc., would stretch forth his arm and drop into the palm of the curtseying gatekeeper—*a halfpenny*!

After Lord Bath's death, his brother and inheritor of his vast fortune, occupied Bath House for three years, when he also departing to the land of shades (Charon got but small tips from these *Adelphi* it may be presumed), the place was let to the Duke of Portland. In 1821, Alexander Baring bought it and rebuilt the mansion. He was created Lord Ashburton fourteen years later, and was the head of the great banking house, which the Duc de Richelieu once said was the sixth great power in Europe. Under the Ashburton *régime*, Carlyle, who was more friendly with Lady Ashburton than Mrs. Carlyle always approved of, was a frequent visitor here. In our days it has been the town house of the millionaire Baron Hirsch, and is now the residence of Sir Julius Wernher, so that it would appear to have always been associated with worldly riches and well-known names.

CLUBS OF PICCADILLY.

At this point begins that remarkable series of clubs for which Piccadilly is almost as famous as Pall Mall; indeed, between the United Empire Club at No. 84, and the Lyceum, at No. 128, there are a good baker's dozen of these "assemblies of good fellows, meeting under certain conditions," as Dr. Johnson defined them. Those in this quarter of the town are for the most part comparatively modern, and I believe I am right in saying that not one of their names will be found included in Timbs' interesting work on "Clubs and Club Life." It would form but monotonous reading to set them all down here, and I should be arrogating to myself by doing so the functions of the compiler of Directories were I to attempt it, but as we go along, one or two will require a word chiefly from the fact of their inhabiting houses which are otherwise interesting.

CLARGES STREET.

Clarges Street, however, for a moment, intervenes before we come to one of them. It was formed between 1716 and 1718, by Sir Walter Clarges, on ground adjoining Clarges House, the residence of his father, Sir Thomas, who, it will be remembered, was the brother-in-law of the great Duke of Albemarle. Like all the streets in this neighbourhood, it is connected with many a well-known name; Mrs. Delany, the friend of George III. and Queen Charlotte; Miss O'Neil, the beautiful actress, who nearly extinguished Mrs. Charles Kemble, and created a *furore* by her rendering of "Juliet" at the Dublin theatre; Edmund Kean, whom no one could extinguish, and who is said to have kept a tame puma in his house; the beautiful Emma Hart, better known as Lady Hamilton; William Mitford, who wrote the story of Grecian prowess, and was himself a Colonel of Militia; Mrs. Carter, that learned lady, who introduced Epictetus to the unlearned; and Lord Macaulay, who remembered everything, and was called by Lord Melbourne "a book in breeches," highly to the amusement of Queen Victoria. These are some of the great ones who have left their record on the houses in Clarges Street.

HALF MOON STREET.

Half Moon Street, close by, which takes its name from an old inn with this sign, one of the many public houses which at one time congregated in this quarter, of which the "Hercules Pillars," the "Swan," the "Golden Lion," the "Horse Shoe," the "Barleymow," and the "White Horse," may be mentioned—was formed about 1730. Boswell once lodged here, and on his own shewing, gave admirable dinners, "and some claret," to such as Hume and Franklin; Garrick and Oglethorpe. Madame D'Arblay's last residence was also here, over a linen-draper's shop; and here, "in a little, projecting window," might once have been seen "all day long, book in hand, with lively gestures and bright eyes," the poet Shelley; so that someone said he only wanted a pan of water and some fresh turf "to look like a young lady's bird, hanging outside for air and song." Here, too, it was, while stepping into her carriage, that the notorious Lola Montes, was arrested in 1849, on a charge of bigamy.

CAMBRIDGE HOUSE.

For a moment a break in the succession of tributary streets, gives us pause to return to some of the more interesting houses in Piccadilly itself; and one of the most noticeable of these is that once known as Cambridge House, but now as the Naval and Military or "In and Out" Club, the latter colloquial designation having its simple origin in the large "In" and "Out" directions for drivers, at its two entrances. This fine house has had at least four names, for, besides those given, it was originally known as Egremont House, and later as Cholmondeley House. It took its first title from the second Earl of Egremont, who died here in 1763 "of an apoplexy, which from his figure was reasonably to be expected," writes Lord Chesterfield. The third Earl, whom Mrs. Delany thought "a pretty man," and even Horace Walpole allowed to be handsome, also lived here for a time. The name of the house was changed to Cholmondeley House when the first Marquis of Cholmondeley was residing here. He had been Chamberlain to the Prince of Wales in 1795, and was, after George IV.'s accession, Lord Steward of the Household; he died in 1827, and some years later the old Duke of Cambridge (father of the late Duke) came to reside here, when the designation of the house was again changed to that of its owner.

Many are the good stories told of His Royal Highness and his habit (like Lord Dudley's) of "thinking aloud," particularly in church—such as his audible remark, when the parson had uttered the words "Let us pray," of

"By all means;" his "No, no, I don't mind tithes, but can't stand half," when the clergyman had read the text as to the expediency of giving half of one's possessions to the poor; and his common-sense view of the non-efficacy of a certain prayer for rain: "No good—shan't get rain while the wind's in this quarter;" and so on.

On his death in 1850, the Duke was succeeded in the occupancy of the house by a man who was also the hero of many excellent "mots"—Lord Palmerston.

"The frolicsome statesman, the man of the day

A laughing philosopher, gallant and gay,"

as Locker-Lampson called him. It is said that much of Palmerston's popularity was due to the splendid functions which took place under Lady Palmerston's auspices in this fine mansion. At his death there was some idea of pulling down the house to make room for a Roman Catholic Cathedral, but happily the scheme fell to the ground, and the place is, with some additions necessary to the club which occupies it, in practically the same state as when the royal Duke thought aloud in its chambers, or the Prime Minister nonchalantly sauntered through its gates.

OTHER PICCADILLY CLUBS.

Passing the Junior Naval and Military Club at No. 96, the Badminton at No. 100, and the massive buildings of the Junior Constitutional, representing Nos. 101 to 104, Piccadilly, we come to a beautiful house, now the home of the Isthmian Club, which removed here from its premises opposite Berkeley Street, now absorbed by the magnificent Ritz Hotel.

This residence, No. 95, was originally known as Barrymore House, having been built in 1780, by Novosielski, for the Earl of Barrymore, on a site once occupied by the workshop of that Van Nost, who was responsible for the statue of George I. formerly in Grosvenor Square. Lord Barrymore was the eldest of those three brothers and one sister, who earned for themselves the unflattering *sobriquets* of Hellgate, Cripplegate, Newgate, and Billingsgate—the second being in allusion to one of the brothers who was lame, and the last, to the sister whose command of strong language was "extensive and peculiar." Gambling and general profligacy—by the way "profligate" might have summed up the whole family—brought Lord Barrymore to great distress, and Raikes records in his Diary that when the peer wished to give a dinner, he had perforce—*à la* Dick Steele—to dress up the bailiffs, who were perpetually in the house, in his own liveries and get them to wait at table!

It is hardly surprising to learn that the house was left unfinished at the death of this unsavoury personage, and subsequently Smirke added the porch. After a fire had occurred here—the curious thing being that it did not happen in Barrymore's lifetime—the place was repaired and opened as the "Old Pulteney Hotel," and here it was that the Emperor of Russia stayed, when the allied Sovereigns were in this country in 1814.

After its day as an hotel, the Marquis of Hertford purchased the house, and greatly improved, but practically never occupied it. This was the third Lord Hertford, who married that Maria Fagniani, about whose paternity George Selwyn and Old Q. could never satisfactorily agree, and who is so largely responsible for the magnificent art collection which Sir Richard Wallace left to the nation.

Next door, divided by a narrow passage, is No. 106, which is now known as the "St. James's Club." Built on the site of an old inn called "The Greyhound," by the sixth Earl of Coventry, "the grave young lord," as Walpole calls him—who, by the bye, married one of the beautiful Gunnings, who killed herself, 'tis said, by trying to improve the loveliness that Nature had given her. Here he died in 1809; his successor to the title also lived here, and, after his decease in 1831, it became the headquarters of the "Coventry House Club" (or the "Ambassadors'"), which was, however, closed in 1854. The house next door is also a club—"The Savile"—one of the literary clubs of modern London. In the old days, it was the home of the famous Nathan Rothschild, who made a great *coup* over the Battle of Waterloo, and once told Spohr that the only music he cared for was the chink of money!

As we loiter along, the trees of the Green Park attract us, and the gradual widening of the thoroughfare as we approach Hyde Park Corner, an improvement made but a few years since, gives an additional effect to the *coup d'œil* that here presents itself. That curious object over there, a sort of high shelf standing on two iron supports, has exercised many a mind as to its uses. Perhaps not many people are aware that the solution is to be found on a plate affixed to the object itself, the words of which are as follows: "On the suggestion of R. A. Slaney, Esq., who for 26 years represented Shrewsbury in Parliament, this porters' rest was erected in 1861 by the Vestry of St. George, Hanover Square, for the benefit of porters and others carrying burdens. As a relic of a past period in London's history it is hoped that the people will aid in its preservation." But we must return to our bricks and mortar and the associations connected with them.

DOWN STREET.

Now we are at the corner of Down Street, which leads directly to Mayfair; and here (in No. 116, Piccadilly) is now the Junior Athenæum Club, but known in earlier days as Hope House, which H. T. Hope, the author of "Anastasius" and the creator of "Deepdene," at Dorking—built in 1848-9, at a cost of £80,000.

When a stranger is brought to this point and shewn the narrow way dividing the club from the adjoining houses, and is told that it is Park Lane (*see page 134*) he probably, being ignorant of locality, receives a shock, having in mind the celebrity of this part of the town and the fine houses which he has been taught to believe exist in it. But this narrow street *is* technically the commencement of Park Lane, and does much to account for the somewhat inappropriate title by which this fashionable thoroughfare is known.

The tenuity of this connecting neck, between Piccadilly and Park Lane proper (if I may so term it), is still more accentuated by the huge block of flats now being erected on the site of Gloucester House, until recently the well-known residence of the late Duke of Cambridge. Formerly this was the town house of that Lord Elgin who is famous as having acquired the marvellous collection of antique marbles over which poor Haydon was so enthusiastic, and here these treasures of antiquity were for a time to be seen. The house took its name from the Duke of Gloucester, who bought it in 1816, when he married his cousin the Princess Mary, one of the many children of George III.

THE GATES OF HYDE PARK IN 1756.
(*From a Drawing by Jones.*)

When Gloucester House was still in existence the two adjoining mansions, Nos. 138 and 139, stood out in the glory of their stone façades, from the old brick house which receded somewhat from the road, but now they in their turn threaten to become dwarfed by the huge erection which towers above them.

These two houses were originally one, and here lived that "wicked old Q."—the Duke of Queensberry, whose manner of life was so notorious. Here the old profligate sat under a sunshade in fine weather to ogle the girls who passed by, and to send by his groom Radford, many an impertinent message to the more attractive of them. Here this "Star of Piccadilly" on one occasion, while engaging a running footman (he was one of the last to keep this former appendage to noble state), made the man put on his livery and run up and down in front of the house, and finding him suitable, told him so, when the rogue replied, "and your livery will suit me," and making a mock bow, bolted, and was seen no more!

It may be well, as we are now at the end of Piccadilly proper (for, although the houses on the other side of Hamilton Place, among which is that famous "No. 1, London," as someone once called Apsley House, where the great Wellington lived, and put up the celebrated iron shutters, now removed, are given in Directories as in Piccadilly, they should more properly be considered as at Hyde Park Corner), to end our perambulation at the house of one who was so pre-eminently a Londoner as "Old Q." I wish we could have done so in better company, and inasmuch as Lord Byron once resided at No. 139, then called, "13, Piccadilly Terrace," we do so, for although his lordship, apart from his remarkable genius, was not a pattern of morality, he compares well with the nobleman whose only redeeming merits were that he was no fool and loved London as he probably loved few things. When in town once in September, a friend asked Lord Queensberry if he did not find it empty. "Yes," he replied, "but 'tis fuller than the country;" and there is little doubt but that even in those early days, no place could have been selected for anyone to better enjoy the life of London than that spot where the tide of humanity met, at the junction of Piccadilly and Park Lane, with almost as full a force as we have seen it do at the corner of Piccadilly and Old Bond Street, where Stewart's, hoary with antiquity (but to-day one of the most artistic buildings in the neighbourhood), stands, and where those keenest judges in the world—our American cousins—love to foregather, on the spot that is perhaps better known to them than any other in London.

The Piccadilly Turnpike, which is such a feature in contemporary prints of this part of the West End, was removed in 1721 from the end of Berkeley Street to Hyde Park Corner. It remained here till 1825, in October of which year it was sold and removed.

THE TURNPIKE AT HYDE PARK CORNER, 1706.

CHAPTER II.

ST. JAMES'S STREET AND PALL MALL.

"O bear me to the paths of fair Pall Mall,
Safe are thy pavements, grateful is thy smell."
—GAY'S "TRIVIA."

Can we do better, after the surfeit of bricks and mortar which we have just undergone, than relax our jaded senses and relieve our wearied eyes by loitering for a few moments in the Green Park? See! it is just across the way, and a convenient entrance helps to tempt our steps. It is not extensive, but it is an oasis that many a Londoner—besides Lord Beaconsfield, who loved to wander there, when he had one of his rare opportunities—will seek with eagerness and enjoy with a thankful heart.

THE GREEN PARK.

When Piccadilly was "the way to Redinge," and before Buckingham House—the red-brick precursor of the present Palace—had risen on the site of Tart Hall, the site of the Green Park was waste land, with here and there a little ditch, and here and there a willow; and yet it has had "its scenes, its joys and crimes," in common with every square foot of ground in the metropolis. We may be sure it felt the tread of armed men in 1554, when Wyatt's rebellion threatened to upset the throne of "bloody Mary"; and a century later, in 1643 to be precise, cannot we in imagination see the crowd of men, women, and children streaming across it to give a helping hand in the formation of those fortifications which were to prevent a king from entering his capital? As to its crimes, it is certain that there were plenty of those committed when the guardianship of the peace was a very different thing from what we pampered mortals are accustomed to consider it. Why, the duels alone that were fought here would make matter for a good-sized chapter. Beau Fielding fights Sir Henry Colt, in 1696, and, they say, runs him through the body before he has time to draw his sword, but, nevertheless, gets disarmed himself; and "That thing of silk, Sporus," as I have already indicated, meets William Pulteney here, some thirty years later, what time the Park had become so favourite a place for such encounters that it is specifically mentioned as "a rendezvous for duels," in a guide to London of the period.

Had Queen Caroline—that clever woman who managed George II. and ruled the kingdom with Walpole—had her way, a royal residence might now be actually in the Park. She did build a library here, practically where Stafford House now stands, but that is as far as she went. Her royal husband, who, with his many faults, was a brave man, and knew how to fight—and on foot, too, as he did at Dettingen—liked reviews of all things, and used to have his troops manœuvring about in the Park on all sorts of occasions. One such review is mentioned in 1747, when "the regiment (Sir Robert Rich's Dragoons) made a very fine appearance, and his Majesty was greatly pleased with them," we are told. The Duke of Cumberland's Dragoons, which distinguished themselves, or otherwise, according to the Stuart or Hanoverian sympathies of the time, in "the '45," were out, for the same picturesque reason, some days later. Then there was that great celebration for the conclusion of the War of Succession, when a huge temple was erected, and fireworks blazed to the accompaniment of a military overture written by the illustrious Handel himself.

Sir Robert Peel wanted to transform the Park into something analogous to what we have seen occurring to the Mall, but surely with less happy results; one of its very charms lies in the fact that in the midst of Urbanism (to coin a word) it remains rustic, in the very centre of conventionalism it is unconventional. The great minister, when advocating such an alteration, could little have supposed that his death would be so closely connected with this spot; but here it was that, riding down Constitution Hill yonder, his horse threw him, on June 29th, 1850, and three days later he was no more.

CONSTITUTION HILL.

This Constitution Hill, about the origin of which name no good explanation is forthcoming, was in Strype's day known simply as the "Road to Kensington," as may be seen on his plan dated 1720.

Here it was that Charles II. was walking towards Hyde Park when—according to Dr. King's well-known anecdote—he met the Duke of York in his coach, just as he was about to cross Hyde Park Corner. The Duke, on being informed that his Majesty was walking, immediately alighted, and going up to the King told him he was surprised to find him on foot and with so few attendants; intimating that Charles was exposing himself to some danger. "No kind of danger, James," replied the Merry Monarch, "for I am sure no man will kill me to make you king." But the road has not always been so safe for kingly heads, for here, it will be remembered, the lunatic Oxford shot at Queen Victoria, as she was driving, on June 10th, 1840.

The wall of Buckingham Palace grounds runs the entire length of Constitution Hill, to which additional width is just being given, and as we wend our steps across the Park, at an angle, towards the little paved way that leads by Stafford House, we can see the commencement of that great memorial which will perpetuate in stone, as they are enshrined in the hearts of the people, the virtuous life and great qualities of Queen Victoria.

Stafford House lies in front of us, to the right. A wondrous pile, it was originally built for that Duke of York whose effigy stands on the top of the great pillar in Carlton House Terrace. Although glorious within, externally—except from its size—it is not imposing, and its plainness gives point to the remark of some wit of the period that it looked like a packing-case out of which Bridgewater House, the graceful building on our left, had been taken.

When Fielding, as we have seen, fought with Colt, he did so in sight of the windows of Cleveland House, which originally stood close by, the ground having been given by Charles II. to that Duchess of Cleveland who caused him so much trouble, and who had a partiality for the Beau who fought beneath her windows.

CLEVELAND ROW.

Cleveland Row takes its name from old Cleveland House, and forms the south side of that most curious of "quadrates," Cleveland Square.

Theodore Hook once lived in the Row, at No. 5; so did Lord Rodney and Sir Sidney Smith; Thomas Grenville, of bibliophilic fame; and Lord Stowell, the great lawyer, and brother of Lord Eldon. George Selwyn died at what was then called, 1, Cleveland Court, in 1791; and Mason, the poet, was residing here at a "Mr. Mennis's" four and twenty years earlier. Walpole and Townshend had their memorable quarrel, parodied by Grey in his "Beggar's Opera," in a room in one of the houses; while Lord Bute, in 1761, moved a portion of the Foreign Office hither from its former *locale* in the Cockpit at Westminster.

ST. JAMES'S PLACE.

The houses that adjoin Bridgewater House to the north are those of which the entrances are in St. James's Place and Arlington Street. The most architecturally noticeable is the first we see, Spencer House, in the making of which, the talent of John Vardy, James Stuart, and M. H. Spong was combined. A little further on is the house in which the poet Rogers lived and gave those breakfasts and dinners which have become historic. The contents were so carefully selected and so rich, as treasures of art or literature, that Byron used to say there was not a single object which did "not bespeak an almost fastidious elegance in the possessor;" and Moore, and Macaulay, and Burney, and a hundred others who were guests here, have left confirmatory praise. Here it was that Byron, invited to meet Moore and Campbell (what a constellation!) would eat nothing but potatoes mashed up in vinegar, and then, 'tis said, went off later to a club in St. James's Street and made a hearty supper off beefsteaks! Here Chantry, the great sculptor, told his host that it was he who, in the days of his probation as a working carpenter, had made a certain piece of furniture in the dining room; but there would be no end to the recollections clustering about this house if I did not place a curb on my pen. Other poets have lived in St. James's Place—Addison and Parnell, besides many another well-known personality; Molly Lepel, and Sir John Cope; Secretary Craggs, and Charles James Fox; "Perdita" Robinson, and Sir Francis Burdett; Wilkes, the noisy demagogue, and Warren Hastings, the great pro-consul.

ARLINGTON STREET.

Arlington Street is hardly less interesting. There is the home of the Cecils, where one great Prime Minister, Lord Salisbury, could once look across the street at the windows of the house that had sheltered another—Sir Robert Walpole. As the son of the latter once wrote to Montagu: "Nothing can be more dignified than this position." In the past, as in the present, its houses have been the homes of the illustrious. The street was formed in 1689, and was the property of that Arlington who was one of the "A's" of the famous (or, shall we say, infamous?) "Cabal." The Duchess of Cleveland withdrew hither, after the death of Charles had made Cleveland House too costly an abode; the Duchess of Buckingham, wife of that Duke, castigated in Dryden's best-known lines, and daughter of Fairfax, Cromwell's henchman; Lady Mary Wortley Montagu, who resided here with her father, the Duke of Kingston; Pulteney, Earl of Bath—as if he could never get away from his enemy, Sir Robert; and Henry Pelham, who lived at No. 17, in the house built by Kent and now Lord Yarborough's. At No. 21 Lord Sefton gave his famous dinners with Ude as *chef* in command; and Lord Wimborne's house, which is already dwarfed by the neighbouring "Ritz," once belonged to Lord Camden, then to the Duke of Beaufort, and was subsequently sold to the Duke of Hamilton for £60,000; while John Lothrop Motley was renting Lord Yarborough's house, from 1869-70, during his term of office as United States Minister.

If we turn back into St. James's Street and look down that famous thoroughfare two things cannot fail to strike us—one, the effective screen at the bottom formed by the picturesque clock-tower of the Palace which dates from Henry VIII.'s time; the other, the marked declivity in the ground, which is only comparable with Ludgate Hill, in the East, and is considerably steeper than any part of Piccadilly or Knightsbridge, in the West.

ST. JAMES'S STREET.

St. James's Street is a street of memories, if ever there was one in London; to mention all the interesting people who have lodged in it would make a very fair chapter; to record even the bare outlines of the history of its clubs and coffee-houses would form another. Appropriately is it named "St. James's Street," for it is pre-eminently *the* thoroughfare of this aristocratic quarter. Here may still be seen one or two old shops that recall Georgian days, although the street is undergoing such a metamorphosis of rebuilding that one never knows but that some fine morning their familiar fronts may have disappeared; here survive some of the most exclusive and best known of the Clubs which are the particular characteristic of this quarter; and the unchanged front of the Palace at the lower end is such a dominating note in the picture, that, looking down the street, when one of those mists so beloved of Whistler give atmospheric mystery to the thoroughfare, we may almost expect to see Charles II. sauntering through its portals with Rochester or Sedley; or George II. driving through its gates on his way to Kensington Palace or Richmond Park.

The history of

"The dear old street of clubs and cribs,

As north and south it stretches,"

is one which, if its record were fully written, would be found to have no little connection with the annals of the country. Its position, its proximity to the Palace, its past inhabitants, its famous club houses (where so much of the history of the country was, and is, evolved,) all make for its claim in this respect.

WHITE'S CLUB.

On our left is the famous bow window of "White's," where the dandies used to assemble to quiz the ladies on their way to the drawing-rooms. What a history has that club! It has been written, and fills two large volumes, and the "betting book" is a sight for gods and men—if not for young men and maidens. In the old days they used to bet on anything and everything, and there is the story of the man who fell down in a fit, outside the club windows, and wagers being immediately laid as to whether he was dead or not, certain interested members solemnly objected to means being taken to revive the unhappy individual—as it would have affected the validity of the bets laid!

White's Club. JAMES'S STREET IN THE REIGN OF GEORGE III Brooks's Club.

It was by giving his arm to one then unknown to fame, from the bottom of the street to the door of White's, that Brummell considered he had rendered a very important service to a young man, and as it were, given him a splendid set-off in life!

The origin of the club, for which, it will be remembered, Horace Walpole once designed a coat of arms, was White's Chocolate House, which was established in 1698, just ten years after Stewart's Bakery, as we have seen, opened its doors at the corner of Bond Street. White's was then on the west side of St. James's Street, five doors from the bottom, and occupied the one-time residence of that Countess of Northumberland, who was such a "grande dame," that her grand-daughter-in-law, the Duchess of Somerset, is reported to have never sat down in her presence without previously asking her leave. It soon became a hot-bed of aristocratic gamesters. Robert Harley never passed by without cursing it, as the bane of half the nobility; Whitehead, in one of his poems, does not hesitate to call it a den of thieves; and although Chesterfield once wrote to his son that "a member of a gaming club should be a cheat or he will soon be a beggar," that teacher of manners and morals practically lived at White's, not putting in practice, it is to be hoped, what he taught by precept.

The Club was burnt down in 1733; but, phœnix-like, sprang up again soon after, at Gaunt's Coffee House, which was next door to the St. James's Coffee House near the south-west corner of the street. Arthur, Mackreth,

Martindale, and Raggett, all names familiar to students of the social life of the eighteenth century, were the successive proprietors of White's, after 1736, when the Chocolate House was formed into a regular club. Nineteen years after that date it was removed to the premises it now occupies and its present outward appearance is due to alterations made nearly a century later.

BOODLE'S CLUB.

Boodle's, another famous club, is almost opposite, at No. 28, and was known formerly, from its gastronomic reputation, as the "*Savoir Vivre.*" The Club House was designed by Adam for John Crunden, in 1765, and additions were made to it in 1821. It was largely frequented by country gentlemen, who knew probably how hard it was "to rival Boodle's dinners," and it used to be said, in consequence, that if a waiter came into the reading-room and called out, "Sir John, your servant has come," every other head was mechanically turned in answer to the summons! Both Gibbon and Wilberforce were members, as was that Sir Frank Standish, caricatured by Gillray as "A Standing Dish at Boodle's." Gillray, by the bye, lived next door, at No. 29, where, in 1815, he committed suicide by throwing himself from an upper window.

CROCKFORD'S CLUB.

Opposite "White's" is the Devonshire Club, which occupies the site of the famous Crockford's, probably the most notorious gaming house of its day. It took its name from one Crockford, who had been a fish salesman in the City, but, coming to the West, made an immense fortune here. The house was built for him, in 1827, from the designs of the Wyatts. The internal decorations were so lavish that the ubiquitous Creevey describes the place as "magnificent, and perfect in taste and beauty," and adds that "it is said by those who know the Palace of Versailles, to be even more magnificent than that," which certainly sounds like thundering hyperbole! The great "Ude" catered for the palates of Crockford's *habitués*, and there is a story told of the illustrious *chef,* during his connection with the club, to the following effect:—Colonel Damer happening to enter Crockford's one evening to dine early, found Ude in a towering rage, and asking the cause, was thus answered by the infuriated *cordon bleu*:—"*Monsieur le Colonel,* did you see that man who has just gone out? Well, he ordered a red mullet for his dinner. I made him a delicious little sauce with my own hands. The price of the mullet marked on the *carte* was 2s.; I asked 6d. for the sauce. He refuses to pay the 6d. The *imbecile* apparently believes that the red mullets come out of the sea with my sauce in their pockets!" Of such are the woes of genius! It was Ude, too, who, on hearing of the last illness of his former patron the Duke of York, exclaimed, "Ah! *Mon pauvre Duc*, how much you shall miss me where you are gone!"

Wellington was a member of Crockford's, though he never played deeply; so was Theodore Hook, who, because his doctor had once warned him against exposing himself to the *night* air, had the following method of abiding by the *medico's* instructions:—"I therefore," he said, "come up every day to Crockford's, or some other place to dinner, and I make it a rule on no account to go home again till about four or five o'clock in the morning!"

BROOKS'S CLUB.

Another famous Club in St. James's Street, was Brooks's, which was nearly opposite the original White's. Like so many of these clubs it took its name from a former proprietor, although it was at first merely a gaming club, formed by Almack.

Brooks, whom Tickell immortalises (if he could immortalise anything) as

"*Liberal Brooks, whose speculative skill,*

Is hasty credit, and a distant bill,"

removed the club from its quarters in Pall Mall to its present position, and opened it in 1778, but, unlike Crockford, he does not appear to have made a fortune out of the concern.

The members included such great ones as Reynolds and Burke and Garrick, Hume and Gibbon, Horace Walpole, Sheridan, and Wilberforce. The latter has recorded his first appearance here, thus: "Hardly knowing anyone, I joined, from mere shyness, in play at the faro table, where George Selwyn kept bank. A friend, who knew my inexperience and regarded me as a victim decked out for sacrifice, called to me, 'What, Wilberforce, is that you?' Selwyn quite resented the interference, and, turning to him, said, in his most expressive tone, 'Oh, sir, don't interrupt Mr. Wilberforce; he could not be better employed.'"

Apropos of Gibbons' membership of Brooks's, a curious memento should still be among the treasures of some lucky bibliophile, for, when Fox's effects were sold, at his death, in 1806, there was included among them the first volume of Gibbon's "Decline and Fall of the Roman Empire," presented by the writer to the great statesman who had written the following words on one of the blank leaves:—

"The author, at Brooks's, said there was no salvation for this country until six heads of the principal persons in administration were laid upon the table. Eleven days after, this same gentleman accepted a place of lord of trade under those very Ministers, and has acted with them ever since!"

There are no end to the anecdotes connected with Brooks's, and the famous or notorious people with whom they are connected. Here is Roger Wilbraham, what time honours were in the air, asking Sir Philip Francis, an absorbed player, what he thought they would give him; and the irate gamester, suddenly turning round and roaring out, "A halter, and be d——d to you!"; here, it is said, the Prince of Wales was a party to the hoax by which Sheridan got elected in the very teeth of the redoubtable Selwyn; here, at a later date, the brewer, Alderman Combe, losing heavily to Brummell who patronisingly said he would never in future drink any porter but his opponent's, retorted with "I wish every other blackguard would tell me the same;" and here is the Duke of Devonshire partaking of that broiled bladebone of mutton for which he had such a passion, and which was regularly prepared for him at the club!

OTHER ST. JAMES'S STREET CLUBS.

Many other clubs which to-day are to be found in this street, are descendants of earlier institutions, while some have taken the place of older ones; among the latter may be named the Devonshire, and the New University, with its noticeable buildings which Waterhouse designed: the former are distinguished by their names alone; the "Cocoa Tree," the "Thatched House," and "Arthur's." Built in 1825, on the site of the original Chocolate House, "Arthur's" took its name from that Arthur whose son-in-law, Mackreth, eventually succeeded to its ownership.

It will be remembered that it was on the occasion of one of the waiters here being convicted on a charge of robbery, that Selwyn remarked: "What a horrid idea he will give of us to the people in Newgate." The Thatched House Club, which grew out of the "Thatched House," where the Dilettanti Society and innumerable other fraternities were wont to foregather, does not stand on the site of the original clubhouse, which was till recently occupied by the Civil Service Club at the corner of King Street; but the name was formerly preserved in "Thatched House Court," which has long since passed away.

ST. JAMES'S STREET CHOCOLATE HOUSES.

Just as the St. James's Chocolate House was the resort of the Whigs in the Augustan age so the Tory headquarters were at the "Cocoa Tree," which was metamorphosed into a club some time in George II.'s reign, and was then noted for high play. There is extant the story of one O'Birne, an Irish gamester, who had won a round £100,000 at the Cocoa Tree from a young man named Harvey. "You can never pay me," said the Irishman. "I can," replied Harvey, "my estate will sell for the debt." "No," said O'Birne, "I will win ten thousand—you shall throw for the odd ninety," which, being done, Harvey, who would seem to have hardly deserved his luck, won! Gibbon, and later Byron, belonged to this club, and this reminds me that it was while lodging in St. James's Street that the latter awoke one morning and found himself famous. An extraordinary medallion portrait under glass commemorates the house (No. 8) in which the author of "Childe Harold" lodged, and it was from here that he set forth to deliver his maiden, and only speech in the House of Lords.

Among other interesting residents of St. James's Street was Charles James Fox; and here Walpole saw his furniture being carried off to satisfy his horde of creditors. To hark back, we find Waller in a house on the west side, and Lord Brouncker, the first President of the Royal Society, living here; Pope at "my lodgings at Mr. Digby's, next door to ye Golden Bell, on ye second Terras in St. James's Street;" Wolfe, who wrote from here in 1758 to Pitt, desiring employment in America; and Gibbon, who died 26 years later, at No. 76, now part of the Conservative Club.

It was in this street that Dr. Johnson once did some shopping with Boswell; calling at Wirgman's toy-shop (at No. 69, where Arthur's is now) "to choose a pair of silver buckles, as those he had were too small."

KING STREET.

King Street, through which we can see the trees of St. James's Square, must not delay us, or we shall never get along, but we may remember that from 1673, when it was formed, to 1830, it was not a street proper at all, but merely one of those exiguous courts, of which Crown Court, in Pall Mall, is a survivor. There is one private house of interest in King Street, for at No. 1c, as a memorial tablet commemorates, Napoleon III., while yet only Prince Louis Napoleon, resided for two years, 1838-40, after he had been expelled from Switzerland. While living here he was enrolled as a special constable during the Chartist riots; and while here he also took part in that famous Eglinton Tournament which required nothing to make it successful but fine weather. It was from King Street that the future Emperor started on his unsuccessful descent on Boulogne, when it is said that he procured a tame eagle from Covent Garden as a sort of political property, which was to be released on his stepping on to French soil—a piece of theatrical legerdemain that cost him the adherence of at least one follower. I may remind the stranger that the famous Willis's Rooms, formerly Almack's, that "Matrimonial Bazaar," as Lord William Pitt Lennox calls it, the laws of which were as those of the Medes and Persians, as the great Duke of Wellington once had reason to remember when he was turned away from its doors, are still in King Street, but turned to other uses, and that just opposite stands the equally famous "Christie's," where old and new masters are continually changing hands.

As we turn into Pall Mall, the picturesque buildings of St. James's Palace tempt us to loiter; but that is a subject which once entered upon in this little book would lead me into an endless maze of historical and topographical *data*, and we must unwillingly pass by.

PALL MALL.

Here we are in the very heart of Clubland; indeed, so long ago as 1849, when J. T. Smith wrote his fascinating book on the Streets of London, he speaks of this noble street as bidding fair to contain in a short time nothing but club-palaces, as he very properly terms them; and to-day (as Thackeray wrote): "Extending down the street palace after palace rises magnificent, and under their lofty roofs warriors and lawyers, merchants and nobles, scholars and seamen, the wealthy, the poor, the busy, the idle assemble."

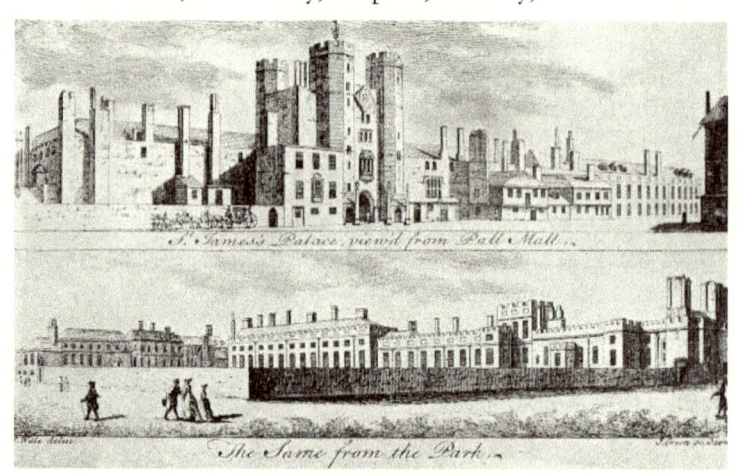

S□. James's Palace, view'd from Pall Mall.

The Same from the Park.

THE CARLTON AND REFORM CLUBS.

Here are the two great political headquarters—the Carlton, founded by the Duke of Wellington and some of his supporters, and built, so far as its premises here are concerned (for it was originally housed in Charles Street close by), in 1836, from the designs of Smirke; and the Reform, which, as its name implies, was started to help the cause of the great Reform Bill, in 1830. The present beautiful buildings of the latter club were the work of Barry, and carry us in imagination to that Farnese Palace at Rome from which some features in its construction were borrowed. The kitchens, as important adjuncts to a club as they are to a college, were designed by the great Alexis Soyer. Among the great successes of this admirable genius (who, by the bye, had been, in turn, *chef* to Prince George of Cambridge, Lord Ailsa, and Lord Panmure), was the great banquet held on the occasion of Queen Victoria's Coronation, and the dinner given to Lord Palmerston, in 1850. In the latter case a gastronomic triumph was particularly appropriate, for "Pam" liked a good dinner as much as any man, and, indeed, an opponent once had to confess that "Lord Palmerston is redeemed from the last extremity of political degradation by his cook!"

THE JUNIOR CARLTON CLUB.

Another great club in Pall Mall, the Junior Carlton, is an off-shoot of the Carlton. Formed in 1864, and originally located at No. 14, Regent Street, the club moved to its present quarters in 1867, when several small houses in St. James's Square and Pall Mall having been pulled down, it arose on their site under the architectural wand of Brandon. Some 20 years later, Adair House was demolished and the club enlarged. Opposite the Junior Carlton, on the same side of Pall Mall (the tiny George Street intervening), is the Army and Navy Club, which has its chief front in the Square. The building was erected by Parnell and Smith, in 1848-51, and is modelled on the Palazzo Cornaro at Venice.

OTHER PALL MALL CLUBS.

Across the way, and next to the Reform, is the unpretentious front of the Travellers' Club, the idea of which originated with Lord Castlereagh about the year 1814. Barry built the present house in 1832. In view of its name, it is interesting to know that one of its rules ordains that no one is eligible as a member "who shall not have travelled out of the British Islands to a distance of at least 500 miles from London in a direct line." When that rule was formed travelling was a very different business from what it is to-day, for now one can hardly overcome the results of a London season without going this distance, and many people find it necessary to go twice as far to keep their minds occupied and their livers in order.

Talleyrand was an *habitué* of the Travellers', and it was here that he made his well-known reply to someone who wondered how a certain great lady could, at her age, have married, as she had done, a *valet de chambre*: "It was late in the game" replied Talleyrand, who was playing whist at the time. "At nine we don't reckon honours."

The Athenæum, at the corner of Waterloo Place, built in 1829, is a very learned club, and appropriately has the finest club library in London. Its premises, which are thoroughly classic, were designed by Decimus Burton.

It had been instituted five years previously by, among others, Sir Thomas Lawrence, Wilson Croker, Sir Humphrey Davy, and that Jekyll, whom George IV., when Prince of Wales, insisted on Eldon's making a Master in Chancery. I will not again inflict the well-known anecdote on long-suffering readers; but I may remind them that on one occasion the hospitality of the Junior Army and Navy, on the other side of Waterloo Place, was, during some cleaning process, extended to the members of the Athenæum, many of whom graced the church, and that soon after, the umbrella of one of the service members mysteriously disappeared; whereupon the irate soldier exclaimed, "Exactly, I knew what it would be when we agreed to allow those d——d bishops to come to our shop!"

Talking of shops reminds me that Hoby's, the celebrated bootmaker's, was, till quite recently, opposite, at the corner of John Street—the shortest thoroughfare, by the bye, in London. The original Hoby was a great character, and said what he liked to his customers, who were legion, and frequently illustrious. He made the Duke of Wellington's boots, and always attributed the successes of that great leader to this fact, and also, parenthetically, to the prayers which he used to offer up on his behalf!

Two examples of Hoby's way of talking to his *clientèle* are extant; one, when Ensign Churchill complained of some boots made to his order, and Hoby, putting on a mock serious face, turned to an assistant and told him to put up the shutters, as if the Ensign's custom was withdrawn, there was an end of the business; the other, when a nobleman complained of his riding boots being uncomfortable when he walked, whereupon Hoby told him that he had made the boots for riding not for walking.

As we are wandering about Pall Mall in a somewhat desultory manner, I make no excuse for turning back from the Athenæum to the large building near by, which up to quite recently, formed an inadequate home for the War Office. That part of it which has a small courtyard in front, in which stood the graceful statue of Sidney Herbert, was rebuilt for the use of the Secretary of State for War; but the most interesting portion is that known as Schomberg House, which was erected in 1650, at the time when Pall Mall was planted with elm trees. It took its name from that Duke of Schomberg who was killed at the Battle of the Boyne, and was much improved by the third and last Duke; but its chief claim to notice lies in the fact that Gainsborough (as Cosway had done before him) lived the last years of his life here, and expired in the second floor room (which is now indicated by a tablet), in 1788, with the well-known exclamation on his lips: "We are all going to heaven, and Vandyck is of the company."

The house next door (to the west), now the Eagle Insurance Office, is interesting from the fact that it stands on the one-time residence of Nell

Gwyn, the gardens of which stretched to the Mall, and here took place that "familiar discourse between the King and Mrs. Nellie, as they call an impudent comedian, she looking out of her garden on a terrace, at the top of the wall, and the King standing on the green walk under it," which Evelyn has thus recorded, and E. M. Ward, R.A., perpetuated on canvas. This site is the only freehold in Pall Mall, and the story goes that on Charles giving "Mrs. Nellie" a lease of the place, she took the parchment and threw it in his face, intimating at the same time that nothing short of "freehold tenure" was good enough for her.

The two adjoining houses have been, not long since, converted into one, and now form the London residence of T.R.H. the Prince and Princess Christian.

When the great "Sarah of Marlborough" was amazed by, as she called them, her neighbour George's "orange chests," she was in residence at the large red brick house, faced with stone, which a grateful nation had presented to her husband (although the Duchess always said it cost him £40,000 to £50,000 out of his own pocket), and which had been erected in 1709, on part of the pheasantry of St. James's Park, which had been leased by Queen Anne to her old favourite. Here the great Duke, "with the tears of dotage" flowing from his eyes, expired in 1722, and one of the great sights of Pall Mall must have been that almost regal funeral which the Duchess arranged herself, and in which figured that funeral-car which she refused at a later date to lend to the Duchess of Buckingham, because, as she said, no one was worthy to be carried on what had borne the illustrious victor of Blenheim! Some fifty years after her husband's death, the indomitable old "Sarah," at the age of 84, was told that she must be blistered or she would die, to which she replied in angry tones, "I won't be blistered and I won't die." She died in the year 1774.

Marlborough House was subsequently purchased (in 1817) by the Crown, as a residence for the Princess Charlotte and Prince Leopold; and here, after the death of the Princess, the widower lived for some years; so did Queen Adelaide after the decease of William IV., and in 1850, the house was settled on the Prince of Wales (now His Majesty the King); but before he occupied it, its lower apartments had been used for various art exhibitions. The entrance is anything but imposing, and is rendered still more insignificant by the high buildings of the Junior Oxford and Cambridge Club next door, adjoining which are the Guards' Club and the imposing front of the Oxford and Cambridge itself, the latter of which was built by Smirke in 1836.

On the north side of Pall Mall we get a glimpse of an almost Georgian perspective if we look up the narrow Crown Court, and can for the moment forget its new front and the adjoining elaborate buildings which have been recently erected facing Marlborough House. This Court is one of the few survivors of many, and is shewn on old plans, which, on the other hand, do not give Pall Mall Place (of later construction), a little further east, which passes under one of the windows of No. 51, once the famous headquarters of Dodsley, the publisher. This house then rejoiced in that sign of "Tully's Head," appearing on the titles of so many of the best-known works of the eighteenth century which the great Dodsley ushered into the world.

PALL MALL TAVERNS.

Pall Mall has been in the past—for you shall seek long enough for them now—noted for its taverns. There was, for instance, the "Queen's Arms," where the sanguinary duel between the Duke of Hamilton and Lord Mohun was planned; and the "Star and Garter" (the descendant of which has but recently disappeared), where Lord Byron killed Mr. Chaworth in 1765, and where the first Cricket Club is said to have been founded in 1774, by Sir Horace Mann (a Kent cricketer and Walpole's correspondent), the Duke of Dorset, and Lord Tankerville, of the Surrey and Hants eleven, and others.

Then there was "Wood's at the Pell Mell" mentioned by Pepys, where, in 1662, Mr. Jermyn and Captain Howard fought a duel; and the "Sugar Loaf," the "Golden Pestle and Mortar," the "Golden Door," and the "Barber's Pole"—to mention but these—were signs that might previously have been seen here. The Coffee Houses numbered among them the well-known "Smyrna" of early Georgian days, and the "King's Arms," where the "Liberty" or "Rumpsteak Club" met and concerted measures against Sir Robert Walpole.

It was in Pall Mall, near the bottom of the Haymarket, that Thynne was murdered at the instigation of Konigsmarck—a brutal deed which may still be seen commemorated on the tomb of the victim in Westminster Abbey; here, too, the mail from France was robbed at half-past eight on January 7th, 1786, almost in the very faces of the Palace Guard, as Walpole relates with natural astonishment; and here the Gordon Rioters were with difficulty prevented from destroying that Schomberg House we have but recently been gazing at.

If great people have left their mark on the street, some curious individualities have also been connected with it. Think of four women racing down Pall Mall for a prize, to wit, "a holland smock, a cap, checked stockings, and laced shoes!" Yet this is what was witnessed here in the year of grace 1733. This appears to have been permitted by the long-suffering authorities, but when one of the residents offered "a laced hat" to be run for by five men, so great a disturbance was created that the magistrates intervened.

During the earlier years of Charles II.'s reign, when Catherine of Braganza came over to share his throne, if nothing else, streets were named with some profusion after that ill-treated lady; thus, as Piccadilly was then converted into Portugal Street, so, for a time at least, Pall Mall was known as Catherine Street. Its former, and present better-known denomination is derived, as all the world is aware, from the game of Pall Mall or Paille-Maille—from Palla, a ball, and maglia, a mallet—a game somewhat analogous to our croquet, which was once played in the "Mall" close by.

CARLTON HOUSE.

Although its name is redolent of Carolean times, it is probable that few streets have been so altered in outward appearance as Pall Mall. The chief cause of this is undoubtedly the favour it has found in the eyes of club promoters, for it is the palatial buildings of these institutions that have chiefly robbed the street of its old-world appearance. But at its eastern extremity, the greatest alteration is due to the demolition of Carlton House, which practically occupied the centre of Waterloo Place at its southern end, and extended east and west with its grounds, entrance court, and screen, where Carlton House Terrace and the Duke of York's monument now exist.

CARLTON HOUSE.

George IV. proclaimed King.

The history of Carlton House has not been written. It is probably just as well that no one has attempted to record the annals of that mansion, for what we know of it from the innumerable memoirs and diaries of the period covering the better part of George III.'s reign and the Regency, is not particularly edifying.

Carlton House was built in 1709, by Lord Carlton, or Carleton, as it was then spelt, on whose death, in 1725, the house came into the possession of his nephew, the Earl of Burlington. Kent laid out the gardens, which extended from Spring Gardens to Marlborough House, at the back of the entire length of Pall Mall, east and west. Lord Burlington presented the house to his mother, who sold it, in 1732, to Lord Chesterfield, purchasing on behalf of Frederick, Prince of Wales. After that Prince's death, his widow resided here till her demise in 1772. Eleven years later, George, Prince of Wales, came into possession, and under his auspices, with the help of Holland, the architect, the place was practically rebuilt, the brickwork being covered with stone, a Corinthian portico added, and that celebrated screen erected, of which Prince Hoare once wrote:

"Dear little columns, all in a row,

What do you do there?

Indeed, we don't know!"

on the site of some houses which had previously hidden the mansion from Pall Mall. (See Plates at pp. 64 and 76.)

Under its new master, Carlton House witnessed many vicissitudes; now being the scene of the most lavish entertainments; anon being practically shut up, when the Prince could not persuade his Royal father to ask Parliament for money to pay his perennial debts, and tried to force his hand by an exhibition of erratic economy; at one time teeming with the gay crowd that formed the Prince's court, when the great Whig families rallied around him, and the beautiful Duchess of Devonshire—"the best bred woman in Europe"—the Duchess of Rutland, Mrs. Fitzherbert, and Mrs. Crewe of the "Buff and Blue" toast, "rained influence"; at another time echoing to the merry wit of Sheridan, the classical allusions of Fox, the broad stories of Hanger, and even the rich tones of the great Sir Walter himself as he joined in the vociferous cheering that greeted the toast of "The Author of Waverley."

If those walls could have related what they heard, many an unedifying tale would have been told, but also the actual truth of many an anecdote which tradition has handed down to us. Did Brummell really tell the Prince to "ring the bell," and did his Royal Highness do so, and order "Mr.

Brummell's carriage"? Did the Royal host become so actually imbued with the idea that he had been present at Waterloo, that he would frequently refer to the hero of that day, with: "Was I not there, Duke?" to which Wellington was wont to reply, with a bow and a grim smile, "I have often heard you say so, Sir?" Did Sir Philip Francis on one occasion go up to the entrance and, instead of ringing the bell, knock loudly on the door with his stick; and did the Prince Regent's confidential friend, Colonel McMahon, subsequently expostulate with, "Upon my word, Francis, you must try and keep Sir Philip in order? Do you know he has been knocking at the Prince's door with a stick, and making such a noise, because he was not admitted, that we thought we should never get him away?"

These, and how many other stories might we not substantiate or otherwise with the help of that mural evidence!

"But the long pomp, the midnight masquerade,

With all the freaks of wanton wealth array'd,"

have passed away with Carlton House for ever, and in its place we have the flight of stone steps leading to the Park, down which a carriage had once rushed headlong but for Mr. Gladstone's restraining hand, and a stone Duke of York gazing at the sky.

The Prince Regent, when he became George IV., thought of connecting Carlton House with Marlborough House by a great gallery running the length of Pall Mall, and dedicated to the portraits of the Royal and notable persons of this country. Had he done so, he would have anticipated the National Portrait Gallery of to-day, and built a nobler Valhalla; but Nash was allowed to demolish Carlton House and cover its site with the great mansions and terraces which now stand there.

The Princess Charlotte—the nation's hope, so untimely cut off—was born at Carlton House, but she is more closely connected with Warwick House, which almost adjoined it on the east side, and stood at the end of Warwick Street, which still exists. The original Warwick House had been the birthplace of that Sir Philip Warwick, whose memoirs of his Royal master, Charles I., are frequently to be met with. When the Princess Charlotte lived here with her governess, Miss Knight, the latter states that the entrance was secured by bars of iron on the inside, and that the Princess was obliged to go through the court of Carlton House. The same lady gives as dreary an account of the house, as Fanny Burney did of Kew Palace; it was, she says, "an old moderate-sized dwelling, at that time miserably out of repair, and almost falling to ruins." This was in 1813; in the following year the Princess, worn out by petty restraints, the coercive measures of the Prince

Regent, and above all her enforced separation from her mother, escaped from the house and drove in a hackney cab to Queen Caroline's then residence in Connaught Place. Hither, however, she returned at the urgent solicitations of Brougham and the Duke of Sussex; and here, subsequently, occurred that scene between the Regent and the Princess and her attendants which forms the subject of a well-known caricature drawing.

It is difficult to pass by Charing Cross and its manifold memories, but if we gave way to the temptation, we should find fresh attractions in Whitehall and the Strand, and I must unwillingly refrain from penetrating further east. The Haymarket, which we are now going up, and Piccadilly east, which we shall presently come to, are, however, both so full of interest that I hope we shall find matter in these "pastures new" to compensate us.

CHAPTER III.

THE HAYMARKET, ST. JAMES'S SQUARE, AND PICCADILLY (EAST).

"A spacious street of great resort."—STRYPE.

THE HAYMARKET.

The Haymarket is one of those thoroughfares whose names speak for themselves. To-day, it is true, it has little the appearance of that which its title indicates, and it is, therefore, all the pleasanter to find its older uses recalled in its present denomination. The curious thing is that the St. James's hay-market, which was held close by, so early as the days of Elizabeth, should have survived to so comparatively recently as the reign of William IV.; yet it was not till 1830, that the Act was passed which removed the market to the vicinity of Regent's Park. That the Haymarket was long an important thoroughfare is evidenced by Strype, who calls it "a spacious street of great resort, full of inns and places of entertainment, especially on the west side."

Let us first see what were the "inns" which clustered here in such profusion that a solemn topographer should have thought it necessary to specifically mention them. The names of some of them have survived, and I find, appropriately enough, "The Nag's Head," "The White Horse," "The Black Horse," and "The Cock," as well as "The Phœnix" (that perennial fowl), "The Unicorn" (that hardly less ubiquitous animal), and "The Blue Posts," one of the best known of them all. If we look at a plan of this locality, dated 1755, we shall see that the west side of the street was riddled with small alleys or yards, some of which were part and parcel of the taverns that once congregated here. Thus, nearly at the bottom, on the site of the Carlton Hotel, was Phœnix Inn Yard; next to it, where His Majesty's Theatre now stands, the yard of "The White Horse"; "The Cock" Yard was about half-way up, and "The Nag's Head" Yard next it. At the back of these, approached from Pall Mall by two streets, known as St. Alban's, and Market Streets, was the St. James's Market itself, since replaced by an extension of Regent Street and Waterloo Place. "Black Horse" Yard was nearly at the top of the Haymarket, where the continuation of Jermyn Street now runs, and practically on the site of the Piccadilly Station of the

Tube Railway; while where Charles Street crosses the Haymarket on its western side was formerly a small passage, known as Six Bell Alley.

"The Blue Posts" Tavern was at No. 59, and was long a favourite resort. Otway mentions it in one of his plays; so does Bishop Cartwright in his diary; and in contemporary newspapers are accounts of those affrays which so frequently disturbed the harmony of these places of recreation.

"The Cock" was probably identical with the tavern bearing this sign in Suffolk Street close by, which Pepys mentions, and which it is likely had something to do with the origin of the name of the adjacent Cockspur Street; while the other taverns must have often afforded refreshment to the various notable people, who once resided in the Haymarket.

One of the greatest of these, who we know loved to take his ease at his inn, was Addison, who, while lodging in an attic over a small shop here, wrote "The Campaign," at the request of the Government. One day, in after years, a little deformed man with eloquent eyes, fired with enthusiasm, brought a friend to this same attic, and mounting the three pair of stairs, opened the door of the small room, and exclaimed, "In this garret Addison wrote his 'Campaign'"—it was Pope pointing out the workshop of genius to Harte.

Among various past notable residents, Sir Samuel Garth stands for physic in the Haymarket; his house, from 1699 to 1703, being the sixth door from the top, on the east side; and histrionic art is well represented by Mrs. Oldfield, who was residing close by, from 1714 to 1726. Garth was a poet besides being a physician, and in the former *rôle* ridiculed apothecaries, about whom he must have known more than most men, in his well-known "Dispensary," a poem which appeared in the year he came to live here. Nance Oldfield, if not of blameless life, was indisputably a great actress, and I believe the only one who lies in the Abbey, where her remains were buried with much pomp and circumstance.

Painting, as is appropriate in a street which to-day boasts a number of well-known picture shops, is represented by George Morland, who was born here in 1763. The inequality of his work is characteristic of the ups and downs of his reckless life; at one time he was producing masterpieces, at another he was dashing off pot-boilers and tavern signs. One wonders if among the latter was that sign which Broughton, the pugilist, hung outside his public-house between the Haymarket and Cockspur Street, and which represented the champion boxer himself "in his habit as he lived."

Nearly at the top of the street on the east side is an old tobacconist's shop (who does not know Fribourg's?) which, in appearance, carries us back to Georgian days, and shows how much has been lost in picturesqueness by the modern methods of shop-building. Wishart's, another tobacconist's, which has, however, unfortunately disappeared, must have looked very much then as Fribourg's continues to do to-day. But the Haymarket has undergone such a metamorphosis that the latter is the only survival of a past day, if we except the portico of the Haymarket Theatre; and now that a Tube Railway Station has invaded the street, the last touch has been given to it in the way of modernity.

It is, however, appropriate that the spot in which Nance Oldfield once lived should be so associated with the "vagabonds" as is this thoroughfare, for here are the Haymarket Theatre, and His Majesty's, which latter stands partly on the site of that Haymarket Opera House, Queen's Theatre, King's Theatre, and Her Majesty's Theatre—to give it all its various names—which most of us remember.

THE HAYMARKET THEATRE.

I will say a word about the Haymarket Theatre first, because it still exists, and by its porticoed front helps to recall the Haymarket itself of earlier days.

The present theatre, as we shall see, followed an earlier one which stood not actually on its site, but on ground adjoining it, as may be seen from an old view of this portion of the Haymarket.

This play-house was originally intended for use during the summer, and in consequence of there being a more important theatre then in existence (on the site of His Majesty's), it was known as "The Little Theatre in the Haymarket." Built at the not extravagant cost of £1,500, by one John Potter, it was opened on December 29th, 1721, by a French Company, who styled themselves "The Duke of Montagu's French Comedians." Their initial piece does not seem to have been a success; and later "The Female Fop" (which Sandford says he wrote in a few weeks, when but fifteen years of age), died a natural death after only a few nights' performance, although it served its purpose in helping to inaugurate the new venture.

Some years later—to be precise, in 1735—the play-house was taken by a company bearing the strange title of "The Great Mogul's Company," and here Fielding's "Pasquin" and "Historical Register" were given. These plays never pretended to be anything but satires, and it is interesting to know that their performance occasioned the passing of "The Licensing Act," which first gave the Lord Chamberlain that power of veto over plays, the exercise of which has been the cause of so much heart-burning ever since; and which, at the time, was the cause of many amusing attempts at evasion, particularly by Theophilus Cibber, one of the earlier managers, and Foote, whose invitation to the public "to drink a dish of chocolate with him" could hardly have misled even the most unsophisticated of country cousins.

For three years from 1744, Macklin managed the theatre, and was then succeeded by Foote, who continued to run the house, off and on, for no less than thirty successful years. With his "Devil on Two Sticks" he is said to have cleared between three and four thousand pounds, of which, by the bye, little or nothing was left at the end of the year. Foote, indeed, had a remarkable aptitude for squandering money, and the motto which he had placed in his carriage: "Iterum, iterum, iterumque," had a new significance given it by his perpetually renewed attempts to replace the money that had taken unto itself wings!

In 1766, a patent was passed for the establishment of a new theatre here, for Foote; and in the following year it was made a "Royal Theatre." Just ten years later Foote sold his interest in the house to the elder Colman, on the apparently splendid terms of an annuity of £1,600, and permission to play as often and when he liked to the extent of a further £400 a year. But although one can understand Dr. Johnson's wonder as to what Colman was going to make out of it, the arrangement turned out well for him, as Foote died within a year, and played only three times.

Colman was succeeded in his management by his son, whose first season commenced in 1790, and who, fifteen years later, sold half his share to Messrs. Morris and Winston. Later, the well-known Thomas Dibdin took over the concern, and it was during his management that, on August 15th, 1805, occurred a great riot here, organised by members of the sartorial trade, who took exception to the performance of a piece entitled "The Tailors, a Tragedy for Warm Weather," as reflecting on their calling. To such a height, indeed, did matters come that special constables and a company of the Life Guards were requisitioned to assist the regular Bow Street officers.

Some years later—to be precise, in 1820—the present play-house, whose historian is the well-known actor-manager, Mr. Cyril Maude—was erected, from the designs of Nash, at a cost of £18,000; the earlier theatre remained open until the larger house was finished, when it closed, on October 14th, 1820, with a performance of "King Lear."

I may remind the reader that such great exponents of the Thespian art, as Mrs. Abington, Miss Farren, Edwin, Elliston, Bannister, Henderson, and "Gentleman Lewis" have all acted at the original house; while the great names of Macready, Webster, and Buckstone, besides Sothern, the Bancrofts, Mr. Tree, and Mr. Cyril Maude in our own days, are among those closely associated with the present theatre.

It was of the Haymarket Theatre that the story is told that that inveterate punster H. J. Byron was once asked (I believe by Lady—then Mrs.— Bancroft) to give a motto to be placed over the pay-office, when he immediately suggested "So much for Booking 'em" as an appropriate heading!

SUFFOLK STREET.

Suffolk Street, running partly behind the play-house, is one of the older streets in this neighbourhood, having been formed in 1664, on the site once occupied by the town house of the Earls of Suffolk. Although the present street is relatively modern, its lines follow those of the older one. At its Pall Mall eastern corner stands the United University Club in its stately rebuilt magnificence, but the street is connected more intimately with Art than Letters, being the home of the Society of British Artists. Once it echoed to the tread of Swift, when he came to visit Vanessa, who for a time lodged here with her mother. Adam Smith was a former resident, as was Moll Davis, for whom the King furnished a house here, before her apotheosis in St. James's Square hard by, as Pepys tells us; and when the Italian Corticelli had his town house here, frequented, in the days of George I., for raffles and assignations, the little thoroughfare must have presented a gay and gallant sight, with which its present-day solemn respectability cannot have much in common.

But perhaps Suffolk Street is chiefly interesting, particularly just now, when Free Trade and Protection are again rivals for our suffrages, as being the last home of Richard Cobden; for here he died in lodgings, at No. 23, on April 2nd, 1865. A memorial tablet marks the house where the great Free Trader breathed his last, and whither he had come only a few weeks previously.

THE OPERA HOUSE, & HIS MAJESTY'S THEATRE.

On the other side of the Haymarket a very important change has occurred, owing to the demolition of the old theatre, and the erection on its the present house, as well as the building of the Carlton Hotel, which did away with the colonnade, once the noticeable feature of this corner of the Haymarket and Pall Mall.

This old play-house, which, as we have seen, went through many changes of nomenclature, was the work of Sir John Vanbrugh, who was backed by a sum of £30,000, subscribed by 300 people, who had in return a right of free entrance to any of the performances. The lovely Lady Sunderland, Marlborough's daughter, laid the first stone, in 1703, the theatre being completed two years later, when it was opened with a performance of "The Indian Emperor," by Dryden. Unfortunately, however, Vanbrugh appears to have thought more of its architectural beauties than its acoustic properties, for not the combined management of Vanbrugh and Congreve (who had joined the poet-architect in the concern), nor the acting of the great Betterton and the company that came with him from Lincoln's Inn Fields, could make Dryden's lines or Vanbrugh's conceits heard even by a tithe of the audience.

The Opera House Colonnade. PALL MALL EAST. Carlton House Screen.

Vanbrugh was succeeded in the management by Owen MacSwiney, under whom an Opera Company, including the famous Niccolini, gave a series of performances here. A year later, Betterton, who had betaken himself to the rival camp at Drury Lane, was lured back and engaged to act for a month with a strong company supporting him. After this the house was again given over to opera, and Aaron Hill became manager, in 1710. He it was who made overtures to Handel to write the lyrics of an opera, the result being "Rinaldo," which the master is said to have composed in a couple of weeks.

In the following year Heidegger, whose name is to be found in the "Dunciad," and who was Master of the Revels to George I.—fancy the solemn Hanoverian revelling!—became manager.

From 1717 to 1720, no Italian operas were performed in the Haymarket, but in the latter year a number of noblemen and gentlemen combined to start a society chiefly devoted to the performance of Handel's works, although Bononcini was also employed, hence arising that celebrated feud between the adherents of "Tweedledum and Tweedledee."

There is on record another great feud between the partisans of the two rival singers Cuzzoni and Faustina, which eventually resulted in the former leaving this country, cheered, if she could be, by some lines by Ambrose Phillips, who termed her the "charmer of an idle age," although the management of the Opera House had not much reason to echo this flattering sentiment.

Later, the opera having fallen into some financial difficulties, Handel and Heidegger determined to carry it on on their own responsibility. From this time, 1734, when Handel's partnership with Heidegger ended, to 1782, the Opera House was the scene of all sorts of entertainments, from Handel's operas and Mlle. Hemel's dancing, to the ball given by the Knights of the Bath, in 1779, and the masquerade of thirty years earlier, when George II. appeared in an "old-fashioned English habit" (an excellent disguise), and Miss Chudleigh, with next to nothing on, reminded the scandalised Horace Walpole of Andromeda, rather than the Iphigenia whom she was supposed to represent.

Some years after the alterations to the theatre, when it was under the management of Gallini, a disastrous fire occurred there, which practically destroyed it, but phœnix-like, a new building quickly arose on its site, although many people, Walpole among them, thought that it was a useless expenditure, as the days of opera appeared to have departed for ever. The new house was designed by Novosielski, and Lord Buckinghamshire laid the first stone, in April, 1790, it being completed in the following year. Later, Michael Kelly and Storace managed it jointly when Sheridan and Taylor were the lessees.

Although principally used either as a theatre or opera house, an innovation was attempted, in 1787, by the introduction of ballets, one of which, entitled "Bacchus and Ariadne," seems to have been anything but adapted *virginibus puerisque*; and it was a question whether the presentation of it or its withdrawal would cause the greater indignation!

The names of Goold, the founder of the Union Club, and Taylor, who was perennially in difficulties, Waters and Ebers, Laporte and Lumley, under the last of whom that great quartette composed of Taglioni, Grisi, Grehn, and Cerito performed; and Smith and Mapleson, are among those who figured at various times as *impresarios* here; while the singers whose voices once echoed through that vast auditorium were such as Jenny Lind and Sontag, Pasta and Tietjens, Mario and Tamburini.

A second great fire, on December 6th, 1867, again destroyed the building, which was subsequently re-erected with its principal frontage in Pall Mall, at a great cost; this in its turn we have seen disappear, and the new "His Majesty's Theatre" rise on its site, with its chief entrance in the Haymarket, and a long frontage to Charles Street. Luckily, the old arcade is embodied in the new building, and here are still to be seen those dear little shops that look so clean and prosperous and yet so diminutive—like a sort of Tom Thumbs among business establishments!

At the north corner of Charles Street and Regent Street is the Junior United Service Club, in which, report hath it, that a certain part of the dining-room, frequented by the older members, is known as "Rotten Row"; while across Waterloo Place (or really the continuation of Regent Street) is yet another Club—the Caledonian—housed in the former residence of the late Lord Waterford.

ST. JAMES'S SQUARE.

A few steps further and we are in the heart of St. James's Square. Here history and legend will run away with us if I do not restrain my pen, for every house has an interesting history; each has been the abode of some famous personage.

Here, in the south-east corner, is the long front of Norfolk House, the residence of the last six Dukes of Norfolk; behind it still stands the old house, used principally as a lumber-room, in which George III., and his brother, the Duke of York, were born, what time the mansion was lent to Frederick, Prince of Wales, by an accommodating Duke. The Bishop of London's official town residence, whither the Duke of Hamilton, after his celebrated duel with Lord Mohun, was carried, is next door, nestling between the ducal abode and Lord Derby's iron-balustraded mansion. Commerce has invaded the Square, for, at the opposite corner, is a Bank, and next to it Lord Falmouth's house, which has some old cannon as posts planted in the pavement before it.

ST. JAMES'S SQUARE IN 1760.

In Lord Cowper's, No. 4, is that magnificent room designed by Lord Burlington, which is a wonder to those who see it for the first time. This is one of the few houses in the Square which has remained in the hands of a single family since the Square was formed by Lord St. Alban's, in Charles II.'s day. Lord Strafford's house is next door; and on the other side it is flanked by Lord Bristol's, another of the houses to which one family has steadfastly adhered.

It is curious, having this in view, and remembering the aristocratic traditions associated with the Square, to find so many of the houses now turned to alien uses. Clubs—the Windham, the Sports, the Portland, the Nimrod, the East India, and the Army and Navy—occupy no less than half a dozen of them; the London Library is housed in a rebuilt structure on the site of the former residence of Admiral, the Earl of Torrington; and an art gallery peers out of the corner premises abutting on King Street.

Members of the great families of Sunderland, Portland, Halifax, Legge, Hyde, Devonshire, etc., besides those I have mentioned, have all resided here; so, too, did the wonderful old Lady Newburgh, who remembered I don't know how many sovereigns, and was a friend of one of the most unfortunate, Charles I.; the first Lord Palmerston, who married an heiress under romantic circumstances; Sir Allen Apsley, who was Treasurer to the Duke of York, and who on one occasion received the future James II. as a guest beneath his roof "for one night only," as they say in theatrical circles; Sir Cyril Wyche, who was a President of the Royal Society; Sir John Duncombe, a former Chancellor of the Exchequer; *and* Sir Charles Grandison; besides Ambassadors from nearly all the courts of Europe.

No; it is to the past that we must turn to find even this most select of Squares in its glory. When all the great houses were standing—Cleveland House (now represented by a huge and incongruous block of flats), Lord Jermyn's fine mansion, on the site of the Portland Club, and Mr. Guinness's residence, and Ossulston House, where the Bank and Lord Falmouth's now stand—an additional distinction must have been given the Square, especially when we remember the great and beautiful residents who were then to be seen in its precincts.

The history of this Square is a particularly fascinating one; but it can be but lightly touched on here.[2] As we have seen, a king was born in its chief house, so, at a later day, a queen was to be observed driving from another residence, that of the notable Sir Philip Francis, to take her trial at Westminster, and a curious print of the period shows Queen Caroline in her carriage surrounded by a vast crowd leaving No. 17, which house, together with its next door neighbour, was subsequently to be demolished to make room for the East India Club.

Another notable residence is No. 20, the only example in the Square, but a fine one, of Robert Adam's work. It was for many years the home of the

Watkin Williams Wynn family, for one of whom it was built, in 1772, until recently, when it passed into Lord Strathmore's possession.

But not always have the residents been of noble birth or irreproachable morals, and as we again emerge into Pall Mall by the Army and Navy Club's gorgeous buildings—the work of Parnell, and standing on the spot where once the famous Raggett, the proprietor of White's, opened the unsuccessful Union Club—we are reminded that in a small house on part of its site once lived that Moll Davis, the actress, whose singing of an old ballad attracted the questionable attentions of Charles II. The footsteps of the Merry Monarch must have often echoed in the Square, where the siren dwelt, and where also lived so many of his friends and acquaintances. Other footsteps have been heard here; those of Johnson and Savage, who, cold and hungry, passed a whole night wandering round the central garden with its statue of King William III. (which was so unconscionable a time in getting itself erected), while they settled the affairs of the nation and dreamed of that immortality which one, at least, was to attain.

By the bye, that open space, formerly a mere rubbish heap, has seen many vicissitudes. Once it had a considerable piece of water within its enclosure, and was octagonal in shape; earlier still it was merely enclosed by posts and rails in a most uncompromising square; to-day it is, to use a much-loved 18th century word, an "umbrageous" garden.

The present inhabitants would be sufficiently startled if Mr. Brock were to suggest a display of fireworks there; but in past days this was a regular concomitant to any great public rejoicings, and many of the influential residents interested themselves in these *"feux d'artifice."* The victory of the Boyne, the capture of Namur, the Peace of Ryswick were some of the more notable occasions for, as contemporary prints assure us, really remarkable efforts in pyrotechnic display.

But we must quit St. James's Square, with its historic memories, its ghosts of the great and beautiful; its houses built by the Brettinghams, Storys, Barebones, and Friths, and decorated by the Adams, the Kauffmanns, the Ciprianis, and the Amiconis of a past day; and to do so let us retrace our steps to its north side, where York Street will lead us into Jermyn Street.

JERMYN STREET.

It is not difficult to trace the name of York Street to the Duke of York, who afterwards became an unpopular king; but it requires some effort of the imagination to connect with Apple-tree Yard, in the same street, that orchard of apple-trees for which this spot was famous in the reign of Charles I.

When the Spanish Ambassador was living in St. James's Square, the chapel connected with the Embassy was situated in York Street, and the building, with the arms of Castile upon it, was standing till so recently as 1877.

Jermyn Street, into which we now turn, is famous. It is as characteristically redolent of the West End as (say) Leadenhall Street is of the East. All sorts and conditions of interesting people have lived or lodged in it; Marlborough, when yet John Churchill, and only a colonel; the Duchess of Richmond, known to readers of De Grammont and students of the later Carolean days, as *La Belle Stuart*; the haughty Countess of Northumberland; Secretary Craggs and Bishop Berkeley, and Lord Carteret; to say nothing of Verelst, the painter, of whose vanity so many stories are told by Walpole. The great Sir Isaac Newton, until he went to Chelsea; Shenstone, when he could tear himself away from his beloved "Leasowes"; and Gray, who, as Johnson said, would go down to posterity with a thinner volume under his arm than any of the great poets, also resided in Jermyn Street. The latter lodged at Roberts', the hosiers, or Frisby's, the oilman's, as he found convenient (paying not more than half a guinea a week for his rooms), just as Bishop Berkeley had done at an earlier day at Burdon's, with its sign of "The Golden Globe."

In the nineteenth century the street may have been enlivened by the jokes of Sidney Smith or the gentle caroling of Tom Moore, for they both sojourned here, the one at No. 81, in 1811, the other at No. 58, fourteen years later. But a greater than either once stayed for a short space in the street; for at one of the many hotels which have flourished and faded here, the great Sir Walter remained for three weeks, after his return from the Continent; and here he lay in that waking dream which had but one dominant expression in its dull monotony, the unconquerable desire to be once again in his "ain hame," and to hear the busy Tweed rippling over its stones.

ST. JAMES'S CHURCH.

In spite of much rebuilding there yet remains one object here which will help to recall us to the past—the Church of St. James's, which fronts both Jermyn Street and Piccadilly. It was erected by Henry Jermyn, Earl of St. Albans, soon after he had begun the development of his neighbouring property. Wren had a hand in it, when it was commenced in 1680, but he concentrated his efforts on the interior, which is extraordinarily light and spacious. Grinling Gibbons was responsible for the beautiful marble font and a portion of the altar; and the organ was originally made for James II. Its rectors have occasionally attained high preferment, no less than three— Tenison, the first; Wake, the second, and Secker, at a later date, reaching the Archbishopric.

Interesting things have happened in this church. Once the minister was ordered not to lay the text on the cushion (as was then the custom) of the Princess Anne, who used to attend here when she was living at Berkeley House, nor "to take any more notice of her than other people," as old Sarah of Marlborough indignantly records; but the rector refused to do this without an order in writing, which the Crown did not think it expedient to give; Defoe was scandalised at the charges made here for a seat, "where it costs one almost as dear as to see a play"; and in the churchyard Gibbon once stumbled and sprained his foot, but he is careful to particularise the time of the mishap, "between the hours of one and two in the afternoon," so that there need be no shaking of heads. Gibbon, who was nothing if not "genteel," selected his church well, for Vanbrugh, in his "Relapse," makes Lord Foppington say that he always attended St. James's for "there's much the best company!"

"THE BULL AND MOUTH," PICCADILLY.

The church and the churchyard in which Gibbon slipped, are so full of illustrious dead, that it would seem, indeed, a difficult matter to pass through them without stumbling against some "pointed clay." Here lies Cotton, who shares the fame of the "Compleat Angler" with his friend Walton; Tom D'Urfey, who made up those "pills to purge melancholy" which so many have found a pleasant enough prescription; the artist Van der Velde, the royal marine painter, who knew the trick of marine painting if anyone did; Dahl and Haysman, the portraitists, and Harlowe, who reproduced the trial scene of Queen Katherine. Mrs. Delany was laid to rest here, so was Mark Akenside, who died in Old Burlington Street; Dodsley, the great Pall Mall bookseller; Gillray, who caricatured a whole generation, and "Old Q," who scandalised another, and so on; while the great Chatham, and Chesterfield—that "glass of fashion"—were both held at the font which Grinling Gibbons had adorned.

PICCADILLY CIRCUS.

If we continue westward along Jermyn Street we shall come to St. James's Street, which we have already traversed, and if eastward, to the Haymarket, which we have but recently left; let us therefore go up the little passage by the side of the church, and find ourselves in the full bustle of that part of Piccadilly which we have till now neglected.

Piccadilly Circus is one of the sights of London. It is the starting-point of at least four great thoroughfares. To the west lies Piccadilly; to the east, Coventry Street, leading to Leicester Square; to the north-west runs Regent Street; to the north-east, Shaftesbury Avenue; while (lower) Regent Street, leading to Waterloo Place, lies south.

"That gentle hill which goeth

Down from the 'County' to the Palace gate,"

as Tom Hood called it, contained several other landmarks which have disappeared, among them, the church on the right hand going towards Pall Mall, and "The Bull and Mouth," at the top south-east corner, whence the "Age" coach, tooled by the Duke of Beaufort, used to leave on its journey westward. Later the "Bull and Mouth" was known as "The Spread Eagle," established in 1820, and now it fulfils some part of its former rôle by being converted into a railway receiving office.

Whether by day, when the flower girls sit around the base of Gilbert's "Cupid," (a "cold pastoral" indeed, in his exposed situation, aiming his arrow at the luggage on the cabs or the passengers on the omnibuses as they pass and repass his happy hunting-ground); or by night, as Yoshima Markino would possibly prefer, when the lamps from the Trocadero or the Criterion are dimly perceived through a fog, or are almost indecently glaring in a clear sky (if ever London has a clear sky above it), Piccadilly Circus is a sight, I always think, to wonder at. It is a perpetual eddy of many waters. If not unhasting, certainly unresting are the passengers on those streams which flow in from so many points and seek so many exits. Here the denizens of Soho emerge to their farthest western limits; here the West End, in electric broughams, comes to the outskirts of its own country. Theatre and music-hall are here "at grips" with their opposition entertainments. Everything comes in time to Piccadilly Circus. The man strolling out from the play in evening dress and crush hat may be hailed by a friend in ulster and shooting boots, whose hansom is the last stage of a journey from the Hebrides or the Himalayas; the east and the west meet here on common ground for that amusement which would seem to be taken in anything but the sad spirit predicated of it by Continental nations.

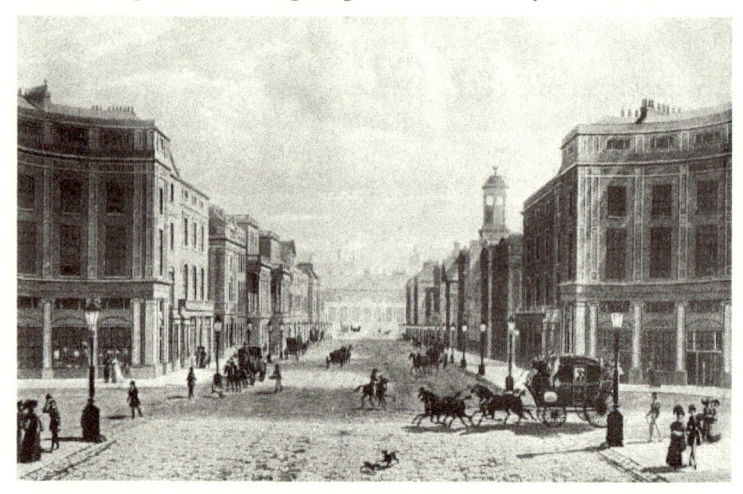

Site of LOWER REGENT STREET, FROM PICCADILLY CIRCUS, WITH
"Bull and Mouth." CARLTON HOUSE AND SCREEN.

And then for the stranger there is such a pleasant commingling of the old and the new at this point. The wilds of Soho, with its historic Square, its streets that defy the most exact logical definition, its church, its memories of Dr. Manette and the sweet Lucy; Leicester Square where once was a royal palace, and the homes of Reynolds, and Hunter, and Hogarth, and our one and only Sir Isaac; and where the Empire, and the Alhambra (awhile the home of that most dreary Panopticon) compete nightly with all the bravery of illumination and gigantic "chuckers out."

In Regent Street, which had its genesis in the Prince Regent's desire for a fine thoroughfare between Carlton House and his residence in Regent's Park, and the making of which did away with as much dirt and squalor as Shaftesbury Avenue has attempted to do in our own day, Nash's magnificent sweep is now, alas! interrupted by Mr. Norman Shaw's splendid "Piccadilly Hotel," the elevation of which shows the design adopted for the rebuilding of the Quadrant. The once famous colonnade has long since disappeared; but in the Haymarket, the Theatre, and Fribourg's delightful old shop still show what it once looked like. And then with these we have the *dernier cri* of His Majesty's Theatre, the Tube railway station, and the roar of the motor 'bus.

If we can but escape from these leviathans of the road, let us beat a hasty retreat from beneath Cupid's bended bow and outstretched leg, and make our way back by Piccadilly to Stewart's corner, from whence we first started on our perambulation.

At the Circus we are nearly on the site of that famous gaming-house, known as Pickadilla Hall, of which the earliest mention appears to have occurred in 1623, when it was in the possession of one Robert Baker, whose widow sold it to that somewhat notorious Colonel Panton, who was associated with Titus Oates, and whose name survives in Panton Street. He it was who built Panton Square, where the Comedy Theatre now stands, in one of the houses of which, in 1762, the Ambassador of Morocco cut off his servant's head because the latter had displeased his sable Excellency in some trivial matter, with the result that the resentful envoy and his retinue received a sound thrashing from an infuriated mob which got wind of the circumstance.

PICCADILLY EAST.

Even in those early days a good deal of trouble was taken to keep Piccadilly, that is, as far as Sackville Street (for the remaining portion was then known as Portugal Street or the "way to Reading"), well paved, and free from contamination in other ways, as Evelyn's Diary and Burton's Parliamentary Journals attest.

By a plan, dated 1720, we can see that then, as now, several small alleys led into, what in the plan is termed German Street. There was on the south side Salter's Court, and—appropriately as being in the vicinity of Pickadilla Hall—Fleece Yard; and Eagle Street and King's Arms Yard between St. James's Church and Duke Street. On the north side Shug Lane is given as on part of the site of Regent Street, and leading to "Marybone Street"; Bear Alley, a few steps further west, probably where stood "The White Bear," formerly known as the "Fleece" Inn, one of the busiest of the old coaching houses, and dating from the middle of the 17th century. Here West, the painter, stayed on his arrival in London from America; and Luke Sulivan and Chatelain, the engravers, both died, the latter only having taken lodgings here on the previous night. And Magget's Lane is given beyond Air Street and close to Swallow Street.

THE "WHITE BEAR" (FORMERLY THE "FLEECE" INN), PICCADILLY.

THE PICCADILLY HOTEL.

(Built on the site of St. James's Hall)

The Arts have been, till recently, well represented in Piccadilly, for nearly opposite to Burlington House, to which we shall shortly come, is the building of the Institute of Painters in Water Colours, and close by was, till the other day, St. James's Hall, where the best of good music was unable to wean the public from their fireside or their theatre stalls in sufficient numbers to make it pay; and so that star-bedizened ceiling and orientally decorated Hall is no more, but is now succeeded by the splendid front of the new "Piccadilly Hotel," the latest, and architecturally the most interesting and original of the many fine hotels that have sprung up in London during the last few years. Indeed, "the Piccadilly," as, I suppose, it will be familiarly called, is, both inside and out, a remarkable example of the palatial character which modern luxury seems to demand in the building and management of latter-day hotels. As I have said, some old land-marks had to make way for it; but what's not destroyed by Time's devouring hand?

QUARITCH'S.

Even Quaritch's, the bookseller's (now removed to Grafton Street), known as well to American and foreign bibliophiles as to ourselves, has been turned to other uses! Who that loves books didn't know the great Quaritch and his top hat, as distinctive as Napoleon's grey coat or Wellington's duck trousers? Indeed, Quaritch was the Napoleon or Wellington, which you will, of booksellers, and Sotheby's his chosen field of battle, where in great contests, he suffered no defeats. That hat, crushed on his head, and so old that it was not to be easily recognised as ever having been of silk, was one day placed beneath a glass flower-cover by a daughter wrought to despair at the inefficacy of repeated admonitions, and the conqueror recognised at last that it had become merely a relic!

With the disappearance of St. James's Hall and Quaritch's, Piccadilly would seem to be losing all touch with past times, did not Hatchard's Book Shop, Fores' Print Shop, Lincoln & Bennett's, Denman's,[3] and Stewart's still remain to crystallise in their well-known names those past days of which, say what we will, we seem to be losing grip with every succeeding year.

THE ALBANY, PICCADILLY.

This fine old house, which has, since 1804, been divided into suites of apartments for single men, was designed by Chambers. In 1770, it was sold by the second Lord Holland to Lord Melbourne, who subsequently exchanged it with the Duke of York for Melbourne House, Whitehall. In Lord Holland's time it was called Piccadilly House, and a previous mansion on the same site had been known as Sunderland House.

DENMAN HOUSE, PICCADILLY.

(The Vignette shows the old building, No. 20, rebuilt 1903).

It is altogether cloistral, and the curious covered passageway running through from Piccadilly to Burlington Gardens, from which suites of rooms are reached, helps to give it that seclusion which Macaulay, one of its most notable inhabitants, delighted in. It combined what he best liked—"a college life at the West End of London." The various suites are numbered in blocks; thus, Macaulay's was No. 1 E, on the second floor, where the earlier volumes of the great history were written; "Monk" Lewis lived in No. 61 K.; George Canning at No. 5 A. Lord Byron and Lord

- 62 -

Lytton both had sets of chambers here, and the former enters in his journal for March 28th, 1814, the fact that on that day he took possession of the rooms, rented from Lord Althorp for seven years. It was from here that he set out to be married to Miss Milbanke on a fateful day for them both, January 2nd, 1815. Lytton, at a later date, occupied the same apartments, and wrote many of his novels here. Lady Lytton once told a friend that she had heard from him that he was here "with Solitude"; but, paying her lord and master an unexpected visit, she found "Solitude" gowned in white muslin and sitting on his knee!

BURLINGTON HOUSE.

Close to Bond Street is shown on the plan of 1720 the large building of old Burlington House. The illustration, taken from an old print of the period, gives an excellent view of it, with its ample courtyard in front and its extensive gardens behind. Think of the site of this being at the time of the Restoration nothing but pasture land! Pepys says that Denham, who wrote those two immortal lines on the Thames, and who is said by De Grammont to have poisoned his wife (who, if such a proceeding could be justified, would seem to have given her lord every reason, by her conduct with the Duke of York), built the house. Denham does not appear to have ever lived in it, however; its original occupier being the first Earl of Burlington, and it was when once visiting him here that Pepys, in endeavouring to seal a letter, set his periwig on fire, as readers of his diary will remember.

The glory of the mansion commenced with the third Earl of Burlington, that munificent patron of art and practical architect, whose praises Pope and Gay and Walpole were never tired of singing. He it was who rebuilt the place essentially as it is to-day, the chief portion of the design being due, however, to Colin Campbell. The semi-circular colonnade which originally flanked the house, as well as the long wall, according to Ralph, the most expensive in England, with its three entrances facing Piccadilly, were taken down in 1868.

When, in process of time, the place came into the possession of the Cavendishes, they sold it, in 1854, to the Government for £140,000. For a time it seemed uncertain to what purpose it would be relegated, and all sorts of suggestions were made. Finally it was added to by new buildings in Burlington Gardens, for the use of the University of London, and by a new façade facing Piccadilly. Now-a-days several learned Societies have their headquarters in portions of the extensive buildings, but to "the man in the street" Burlington House spells the Royal Academy, the council of which obtained a lease of their building in 1866.

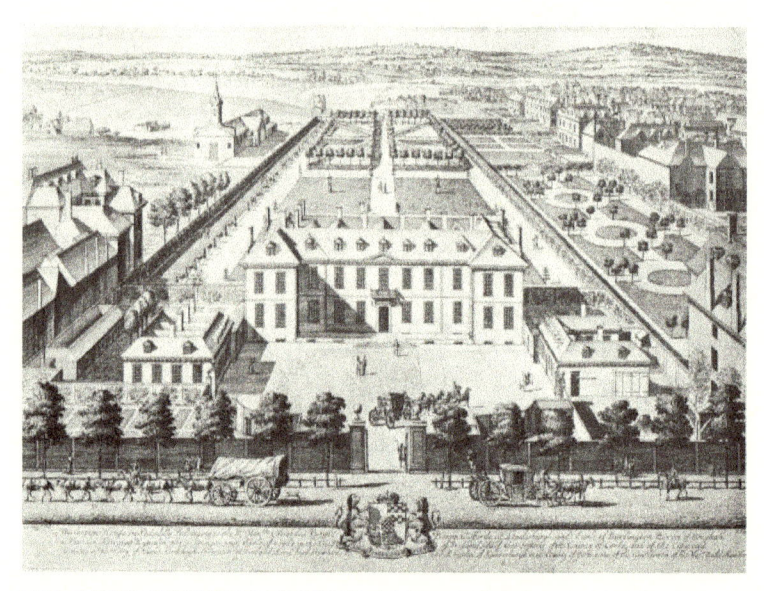

OLD BURLINGTON HOUSE AND GARDENS, PICCADILLY.

Now let us find our way back again to Piccadilly by the easy route, especially in wet weather, of the Burlington Arcade—a sort of *Passage des Princes* of London—designed for Lord George Cavendish, in 1818, which tradition says was originally intended as a covered court to prevent dirt and rubbish from being thrown on the walks of Burlington House gardens.

One could, of course, go loitering over reams of paper in Piccadilly, for nearly every house or its site has had a history; every stone has echoed the footsteps of the illustrious and interesting for many a generation. All the great pageants of London have passed between its shops and houses into the night. And now, as we turn into the bustle of its chief and richest artery, let us exclaim with Phil Porter:—"Farewell, my dearest Piccadilly."

CHAPTER IV.

BOND STREET.

*"And now our Brothers Bond Street enter
Dear Street of London's charms the centre."*
—LYTTON.

BOND STREET.

Bond Street is really as much the centre of the charms of London to-day, as it was when Lord Lytton wrote the lines quoted above; if by charms we mean fine shops, about which Lord Beaconsfield once waxed eloquent, and a segregation of brilliant humanity; otherwise it is curious that a thoroughfare of such importance should be at once so narrow and so cut up by tributary streets, in some cases, wider than it is itself, which make it crowded and inconvenient to a degree only possible in a City as old and as relatively unchanged in outline as London; for Bond Street, although not of any great age, as we understand the word, would probably be considered by those not so familiar as ourselves with antiquity, as having a decent pedigree, for it dates from 1686, and forms perhaps the most important portion of the scheme of development associated with Sir Thomas Bond.

It occupies a part of the site of Clarendon House, and when that mansion with its grounds of 300 acres was purchased by Bond and others, the street was formed. The west side was the first to be built, being then termed Albemarle Buildings, from the Duke of Albemarle who sold Clarendon House to Bond. Hatton described the street in its early days as being "inhabited by the nobility and gentry." You shall seek long enough to-day before you find members of either class represented among the inhabitants other than occasionally in the various hotels in the street, or perhaps in chambers above the shops, which is but a repetition of what was the custom at an earlier day, when all sorts of illustrious individuals gave as their addresses the upper parts of business premises which, in the absence of numbers to houses and shops, were sufficiently distinctive; thus, when we read of (say) the "Duke of A., at Mr. Jones's, hairdressers," we are not to assume that that capillary artist entertained noble guests in his first floor front, other than in the light of lodgers who paid handsomely for the privilege of being in a fashionable street without having to keep up a fashionable house. But, at first, private houses were as much *de rigueur* in Bond Street as they are in Brook Street or Grosvenor Street to-day, and one of the earliest titled inhabitants was that Duke of St. Albans, the son of Charles II. and Nell Gwynn, whose title would seem to have been a royal afterthought, according to the well-known story, which tells us that, on one occasion, his mother addressed him as "little bastard," when Charles, who overheard it, remonstrated with her for the use of the term, whereupon Mistress Eleanor, who probably used the ugly word for a sufficiently good reason, replied that the child had no other name. This, apparently, set the King a-thinking, with the result that shortly afterwards, a patent of nobility was made out for the boy. Although I can't say in what year the Duke took up his residence here (it was probably about 1720), he died in 1726, and an advertisement in *The London Gazette* in the following year contains an intimation to the effect that his Grace's house was then for disposal, in consequence of his decease.

The *Court Guide* is responsible for the names of other inhabitants, and among them may be noted that Duke of Kingston who married a painfully notorious wife—Miss Chudleigh; and that Countess of Macclesfield who proved such an unnatural mother to Savage, the poet.

In 1708, I find Lords Abingdon, Anglesea, and Coningsby mentioned as living in Old Bond Street; some years later the Countess of Gainsborough resided here; but the street as a residential quarter is more interesting from the fact that Laurence Sterne died, at what is the present No. 41, in 1768. The man whose name was on everyone's lips, and whose extraordinary work was in everyone's hands, departed to the land of shades with only two hirelings to bid him Godspeed; and one of these alien hands, that of John Macdonald, a footman, has left the description of that last strange scene. "About this time Mr. Sterne, the celebrated author, was taken ill at the silk-bag shop in Old Bond Street.... I went to Mr. Sterne's lodgings; the mistress opened the door; I inquired how he did. She told me to go up to the nurse; I went into the room, and he was just a-dying. I waited ten minutes; but in five he said, 'Now it is come'! He put up his hand as if to stop a blow, and died in a minute."

LONG'S HOTEL, BOND STREET.

The ubiquitous Boswell was lodging in Old Bond Street a year after Sterne's death, and Pascali Paoli, whose name looms largely in Boswell's "voluminous page," had already come here some eight years earlier. Gibbon, on his return from Lausanne, also lodged in Bond Street, where he writes: "While coaches were rattling through Bond Street, I have passed many a solitary evening in my lodgings with my books"; while half a century earlier Mrs. Loe, a friend of Lady Wentworth's, was residing here, in 1710, and we find the old gossip visiting her and subsequently informing her son that "she (Mrs. L.) had ten wax candles, six in one room and fower in a very little one and very fynly furnished," to her ladyship's evident astonishment.

At No. 24, the Artists' Benevolent Institution was housed, in 1814; but this particular building is more interesting still from the fact that, in 1791, it was the residence—one of his many in London—of Sir Thomas Lawrence; while Northcote, the artist, at No. 2, in 1781, and Ozias Humphrey, the miniature painter, at No. 13, in 1796, combine with Lawrence, to represent Art here.

Bond Street, if to a lesser degree than some other thoroughfares close by, has always been noted for its hotels, one of the most famous being Long's, at Nos. 15 and 16, rebuilt and greatly enlarged in 1888, which was patronised by Sir Walter Scott; and here he met Lord Byron for the last time in 1815; and Stevens's Hotel, two doors off, where Byron was to be met with in the days when he affected to live a fashionable life and consort with the "Dandies." Stevens's was at No. 18, and, having been rebuilt in 1888, is now a jewellers'; another hostelry has also disappeared these 30 years—this was the Clarendon Hotel, at No. 169, which occupied the former town residence of the Dukes of Grafton, where at a later time the great Chatham once lived.

Old Bond Street, which begins at "Stewart's Corner," runs into New Bond Street with nothing to mark their division or to indicate that they form, except in name, anything but one continuous thoroughfare. The latter was not, however, formed till about 30 years after its prototype; but it equals it in interest by reason of the illustrious ones who have dwelt in it. Here, for instance, came in 1727, to lodge with his cousin Lancelot, at a house then described as "over against the Crown and Cushion," the great Dean of St. Patrick's, whom we have met with in Piccadilly when he was lodging in Pall Mall or Bury Street; here lived a few years later that most delightful of garrulous memoir-writers, Mrs. Delany, the friend of Fanny Burney and Queen Charlotte and of how many others; Lord Coventry, who married one of the beautiful Gunnings, was here, in 1732; so was Lord Craven and Lord Abergavenny; later still George Selwyn cut his jokes in the street and hurried by this way to many a last scene at Tyburn, not far off in the Oxford Road. Dr. Johnson's ponderous form might have been seen here, rolling along, as he touched all the posts he passed.

Thomson, "who sang the seasons and their change," and used to lie abed so unconscionable a time o'mornings also lived in New Bond Street, before he flitted to "ambrosial Richmond."

Not only have men of thought and fashion resided here, but men of action, in the persons of Lord Nelson and Sir Thomas Picton, have been represented. The former was staying at No. 147, in 1797, and therewith a curious circumstance is on record. After he had been created Duke of Bronté, he was accustomed to make presents to his friends of casks of Marsala, for which his estates in Sicily were celebrated. Curiously enough, during some excavations next door to Nelson's one-time residence, a cask of this wine, in a bricked-up cellar, was discovered. So rotten, however, had the cask become, that on exposure to the air it fell to pieces.

Southey tells of the following incident which occurred during Nelson's sojourn here.

"One night, after a day of constant pain, Nelson retired early to bed ... the family was soon disturbed by a mob knocking loudly and violently at the door. The news of Duncan's victory had been made public, and the house was not illuminated. But when the mob was told that Admiral Nelson lay there in bed, badly wounded, the foremost of them made answer, "You shall hear no more from us to-night.""

Sir Thomas Picton, who fell at Waterloo, was living in Bond Street at the same time that Nelson and Lady Hamilton were there, and a few years later we find the redoubtable Lord Camelford a resident at No. 148. His rooms were so typical of those of a man about town of the day, that Cruickshank introduced the interiors in his illustrations to Pierce Egan's "Tom and

Jerry"; while the authors of the "Rejected Addresses" have also left on record an enumeration of the various lethal weapons that decorated the walls.

Lord Camelford was one of those fire-eaters who never seem able to exist for any length of time without "entrance to a quarrel." He was known and feared throughout the town, and few cared to tackle the man who was so ready to seek an occasion for fighting, and so deadly in the field. It is thus that the best stories told of him are those which relate his encounters with strangers, one of which I will give, in the words of Timbs, who collected much interesting data about Lord Camelford's career.

"Entering one evening the Prince of Wales's Coffee-house in Conduit Street, Lord Camelford sat down to read the papers. Soon after came in a conceited fop, who seated himself opposite his Lordship, and desired the waiter to 'bring a pint of Madeira and a couple of wax candles and put them into the next box.' He then drew to himself Lord Camelford's candle and began to read. His Lordship glanced at him indignantly and then continued reading. The waiter announced commands completed, when the fop lounged round into the box and began to read. Lord Camelford then, mimicking the tone of the coxcomb, called for a pair of snuffers, deliberately walked to the next box and snuffed out both the candles, and returned to his seat. The coxcomb, boiling with rage, roared out, 'Waiter, who is this fellow that dares thus to insult a gentleman? Who is he? What is he? What do they call him?' '*Lord Camelford*, sir,' replied the waiter. 'Who? Lord Camelford!' returned the fop, in a tone of voice scarcely audible, terror-struck at his own impertinence. 'Lord Camelford! What have I to pay?' On being told, he laid down the money and stole away without daring to taste his Madeira!"

"THE WESTERN EXCHANGE," BOND STREET.

It was while living in Bond Street that Lord Camelford chose to ignore the general illuminations for the peace of 1801, and would allow no lights to shine in the windows of his rooms. The result was that the mob attacked the house, and proceeded to break all the windows, whereat the pugnacious peer, undaunted, sallied forth with a thick stick, and proceeded to lay about him to such good effect that it was not till a considerable space of time had elapsed that he was overpowered by numbers, and was, perforce, constrained to retreat in an almost unrecognizable and wholly undignified condition.

To-day Bond Street, Old and New, is as nearly a complete street of shops as any in London; indeed, it is pre-eminently the "street of beautiful shops," as Mr. Meredith calls it, and is, in this connection, known throughout the world. Anyone walking down it would have to draw heavily on his imagination, if he would try to realise that, as Bramston writes:— "Pease, cabbages, and turnips once grew where now stands New Bond Street ...", so completely has time metamorphosed this once rural spot into a promenade of bricks and mortar, where the ends of the world seem to have been ransacked to fill its marts with all the riches of Nature and Art conceivable by the mind of man.

The shops of Bond Street have always been famous. In the early years of the 19th century the so-called Western Exchange was established there, but has long since disappeared. Its size can be estimated by the illustration here given, taken from an old coloured print of the day.

But undeniably fashionable and central as is Bond Street, the stranger will be struck at its exceeding tenuity, especially in that part where Grafton Street joins it. Here, during the season, one is accustomed to see carriages and carts in apparently inextricable confusion, until the white glove of authority is raised aloft and confusion ceases to be confounded.

Lord Beaconsfield, who knew and loved his London thoroughly, once wrote that, "Those who know Bond Street only in the blaze of fashionable hours can form but an imperfect conception of its matutinal charm when it is still shady and fresh, when there are no carriages, rarely a cart, and passers-by gliding about on real business."

Should, then, we wish to feel "as in some Continental city," which the author of "Endymion" assures us is the case, if we share Bond Street with the lark, we must join this blythe spirit, before the late breakfasted "West End" surges through its long vista.

One of the street's former residents, we may be sure, never did this, for, when the poet Thomson was lodging at a milliner's here, he, to use Mrs.

Piozzi's words, "seldom rose early enough to see the sun do more than glisten on the opposite windows of the streets."

BURLINGTON STREET AND BURLINGTON GARDENS.

Burlington Gardens, leading to Old Burlington Street, and, by Vigo Street, to Regent Street, is the first thoroughfare we come to on the right after leaving Piccadilly. Old Burlington Street has passed through no less than three changes of name. In 1729 it was known as Nowell Street; four years later it blossomed into Great Burlington Street; to-day this adjective is, appropriately, discarded. It, of course, takes its name from Lord Burlington, whose palace stood between Burlington Gardens and Piccadilly, and whose grounds once occupied the land where the street now runs. The West End branch of the Bank of England is housed in Burlington Gardens in the residence formerly known as Uxbridge House, from the lesser title of that Marquis of Anglesea who once owned it, and who died here, in 1854. Famous for his share in the victory of Waterloo, one of his legs lies buried in the little church adjoining the battle field, and the old soldier was once surprised, on paying it a subsequent visit, to find the resting place of his limb converted into a sort of shrine. Uxbridge House was erected in 1790-2 by Vardy and Bonami, and stood on the site of Queensbury House, where Gay's patron and patroness, who set up that great monument to the poet, in Westminster Abbey, once lived.

Another titled lady, whose connection with a poet has alone caused her name to survive, resided in Burlington Street, in the person of Lady Warwick, the widow of the great Addison; and among other past inhabitants mention may be made of Lord Hervey (Pope's "Sporus" and "Lord Fanny"); Mark Akenside, the poet-physician, who died here in 1770; and Sir Joseph Banks, who took a house here in the following year; Colonel Ligonier (whose portrait by Reynolds is one of that Master's memorable achievements), and the Marquis Cornwallis, who resided at No. 29, where he died in 1805.

Another great soldier is indirectly connected with the street, for we find Wolfe writing to his mother and brother who were at one time living here, although there is no evidence to show that the hero of "The Heights of Abraham" himself ever resided in Burlington Street. The "great" Lady Cork—for I think she deserves the adjective—is, however, closely associated with this street. That noble patroness of literature, and last of the "blue stockings"—to use the words in their best sense—died here, in 1840, and Hayward has recorded the charm of her personality, her good nature, and unusual gifts.

It is an interesting fact that in Burlington Street brass door-plates bearing the names of private persons (of which Lord Powis's in Berkeley Square is the sole survivor) were first used in London.

VIGO STREET.

Vigo Street, which connects Burlington Gardens with Regent Street, takes its name from the sea-fight which occurred at Vigo Bay in 1702. It was formerly known as Vigo Lane, which title was originally applied to that portion of the thoroughfare now known as Burlington Gardens, as well. The change seems to have taken place subsequently to the formation of Regent Street.

CLIFFORD STREET.

A few steps further up Bond Street, we come to Clifford Street, where Dr. Addington, the father of Lord Sidmouth, lived, at No. 7. Lord Sidmouth himself, who was, in consequence of his father's profession and also because he once prescribed a soporific for George III., known as "the Doctor," also dwelt here, and was, at least on two occasions, visited here by Lord Nelson. Bishop Hurd, known both ecclesiastically and also for his edition of Horace, also once resided close by, at No. 5; and Sir Arthur Wellesley was staying at No. 14, in 1806; while the Prince of Orange, who came to this country with the object of becoming engaged to the Princess Charlotte—an object frustrated by the Grand Duchess of Oldenburg, as well as by the Princess's almost open repugnance to the not very prepossessing gentleman himself—lodged at his tailor's, at No. 8.

The street also once had its particular Coffee-house (as what street in London in those days had not?), known as the "Clifford Street Coffee-house," which is chiefly interesting from the fact that the "Debating Club," of which "Conversation" Sharp and Lord Charles Townshend were shining lights, once had its headquarters here.

SAVILE ROW.

Clifford Street leads into Savile Row, named after Dorothy, the heiress of Savile, Marquis of Halifax, and wife of the architect Earl of Burlington. Here Lady Suffolk, Queen Caroline's "good Howard," and most respectable of Royal mistresses, lived, in a house she had purchased for £3,000, in 1735. William Pitt and his brother were also residing in Savile Row in 1781, and here died, under the pathetic circumstances known to all the world, Richard Brinsley Sheridan, at No. 17, whence he wrote to Rogers that agonizing letter for assistance to prevent the bailiffs "putting the carpets out of window," as the dying man phrased it. A tablet indicates the last home of "Sherry," who had enlivened a generation with his wit and astonished it by his surprising gifts.

Among other residents at a later date, at No. 20, was Bobus Smith, the brother of Sydney; and Grote, the historian of Greece, who died, at No. 12, on June 18th, 1871. Here Mrs. Grote gave those musical receptions at which the voice of Jenny Lind and the recitals of Chopin and Thalberg were to be heard. A memorial tablet now indicates Grote's residence here.

Sir Benjamin Brodie, the great surgeon, was at one time living at No. 16, Savile Row, and Tierney, the politician, drew his last breath at No. 11, in 1830.

CORK STREET.

Cork Street, joining Clifford Street and Burlington Gardens, was named after Richard Boyle, Earl of Cork, and its chief feature was the fine house, or, rather one should perhaps say, externally fine house, for Walpole affirms that "all its beauty was outside"—which Lord Burlington designed, in 1723, for Field-Marshal Wade, on whose death, in 1748, it was sold by public auction.

In Cork Street lived Dr. Arbuthnot, the friend of Pope and Swift, and one of the three "Yahoos of T'witnam"; he appears to have come here in 1729, and here he died six years later. Another one-time resident was Mrs. Abigail Masham, who replaced Sarah of Marlborough in the affections and confidence of Queen Anne.

Cork Street has always been notable for its hotels, from the time when Gibbon speaks of the Cork Street Hotel, to the later days of the Burlington, where the Empire-builder, Cecil Rhodes, was wont to put up.

CONDUIT STREET.

Conduit Street can be reached from Savile Row by one the quaintest little alleys in the West End, called Savile Place, a tiny thoroughfare which I never go through without expecting to see a Sedan chair waiting at the other end, and a bewigged and beeswonded gentleman or a hooped and patched lady passing through on their way to it. If we followed them we should find ourselves in the middle of Conduit Street, but, as for my purpose it is more convenient to enter at its western end, let us pass along Bond Street until we come to this its largest tributary.

The width of Conduit Street is accounted for when we know that it originally consisted of private houses, although you shall seek long enough nowadays ere you find one that has not been transformed into a business establishment of some sort or another. The street was completed in 1713, and takes its name from a conduit of water which stood in what was then known as Conduit Mead, a field of 27 acres, described in the vaguest of vague ways as lying between Piccadilly and Paddington, and of which Lord

Clarendon had obtained in 1666 a lease of 99 years at the nominal rental (oh! those rents of former days, are they not alone sufficient to stamp that far-gone period as the "good old times"?) of £8 per annum.

The Chapel of the Trinity, which had been built by Archbishop Tenison, in 1716, and replaced the older wooden chapel, once used by James II. on Hounslow Heath, when his camp was pitched there, but subsequently brought hither and left stranded in what now seems somewhat incongrous surroundings, was standing so late as 1877; but its site has now given place to one of the many tailors' establishments for which Conduit Street is noted. Evelyn, in an entry in his diary for July 18th, 1691, mentions attending service at the original chapel, then but newly arrived here from Hounslow. One can with difficulty imagine the place surrounded by those fields in which Carew Mildmay, according to Pennant, remembered shooting woodcock, and before Lord Burlington, the first to build here, had set about the development of the property. When, however, houses *were* erected, they soon found illustrious tenants. The Earls of Macclesfield had their town residence at what is now No. 9 and to-day the headquarters of the Royal Society of British Architects, and other Societies. The notorious Duke of Wharton was also living here, in 1725; so were Boswell and Wilberforce at later dates. One wonders if it was in Conduit Street that poor Sheridan was once found drunk, but, so far as speech was concerned, anything but incapable, and when asked by the Watch whom he might be, hiccuped out, "William Wilberforce"! Delmé Redcliffe died in this street; and at 36, resided Sir Walter Farquhar, the physician whose name has come down to posterity chiefly through the fame of one of his patients, the great William Pitt. Farquhar was not the only doctor of note whose address was in Conduit Street, for Sir Astley Cooper died here, at No. 39, in 1841, and that Dr. Eliotson who once saved Thackeray's life (and to whom in consequence the novelist dedicated "Pendennis"), lived at No. 37, a house doubly famous (though since rebuilt), having been the residence of George Canning, for a year, as a memorial tablet testifies. But the chief interest in the street, lies in the fact that here, on January 24th, 1749, was born Charles James Fox, perhaps the most remarkable of all the remarkable men who made the later years of George III.'s long reign memorable.

The street had, of course, its taverns or coffee-houses; notably, "The Prince of Wales's," where David Williams inaugurated the Royal Literary Fund, in 1772, the year in which Boswell came to lodge here, and the scene of the last of those quarrels which Lord Camelford was never tired of provoking. This terrible fire-eater seems to have at last met more than his match (at one time it was generally supposed that he never would do so) in a Captain Best, and as the result of a dispute about a lady of easy ethics named Simmons, the two went away to the fields behind Holland House, and fought the last duel in which Camelford was ever to take part, in the year of grace 1804. His Lordship had at an earlier date, wantonly insulted the great traveller Vancouver, in the same street; and there was therefore a sort of poetic justice in the coincidence that he should forfeit his life as the result of one more dispute in this locality.

Another tavern in the street had also a gruesome notoriety, for it was from "The Coach and Horses" that Thurtell, the cold-blooded murderer of Weare, drove in that gig, made famous by Carlyle's celebrated allusion, to pick up and drive into the country his "murdered man"—to apply Keats's magnificent anticipatory phrase.

MADDOX STREET.

To the north of Conduit Street we come to Maddox Street, one of those formed by the Earl of Burlington as part of his building development, in 1721. It takes its curious name from that of the original ground landlord, Sir Benjamin Maddox, who died in 1670.

GEORGE STREET.

The chief thoroughfare running through Maddox Street is George Street, connecting Conduit Street with Hanover Square.

First named Great George Street in honour of King George I., it was formed about 1719, and, apart from its many past inhabitants of light and leading, is known all the world over as containing that church of St. George's, Hanover Square, which has always been associated with the weddings of fashion.

ST. GEORGE'S, HANOVER SQUARE.

It was one of the fifty churches which were ordered to be erected in Queen Anne's reign, and was commenced during the last year of her rule. It either took an unconscionable time in building or its erection was delayed, for it was not consecrated till 1724. James of Greenwich, as he is called, was the architect, and even Ralph, who wrote a sort of gossiping survey of London, and is so hypercritical that hardly anything in the metropolis wholly pleases him, unreservedly praises the elevation of its Corinthian portico and its lofty clock-tower. The interior is not particularly striking, but the marriage-registers are of the greatest interest and importance. Here will be found the names of the Duke of Kingston and Miss Chudleigh, who were married in 1769, the lady already being the wife of Mr. Hervey, and afterwards figuring in that celebrated bigamy case, about which most of us have read or heard. Three years after this wedding, we find the great miniature painter, Richard Cosway's name opposite that of Marion Hatfield, who, as Mrs. Cosway, also made some mark as a painter of portraits "in little."

Twenty years later Sir William Hamilton leads to the altar Emma Hart, whose name is as closely associated with the fame of Nelson and the genius of Romney as with that of her lawful lord; while at least one member of the Royal family has been married in St. George's; for here, in 1793, the Duke of Sussex was united to Lady Augusta Murray, a marriage rendered void by the Royal Marriage Act.

Among other names which may be picked out from an almost inexhaustible list, are those of the Earl of Derby, who, on the death of his first wife, married in somewhat indecent haste, the beautiful and talented actress, Miss Farren, although the actual ceremony was performed at his Lordship's house in Grosvenor Square; Mr. Heath, who was united here to the notorious Lola Montes, for whose "*beaux yeux*," a king of Bavaria almost lost his throne; and Mr. Cross, who was married, in 1880, to Miss Evans, known to all readers as George Eliot.

George Street, Continued.

George Street, as well as Hanover Square, has in latter days taken on itself a certain business and commercial air, sadly at variance with its past traditions, for where we now find offices, and particularly dressmakers' headquarters, once dwelt people of fashion, and some of national importance. For instance, No. 25, with its fine stone front, erected for Earl Temple in 1864, and later the residence of the Duchess of Buckingham, was, before its transformation a smaller house in which lived successively John Copley, the painter of the well-known "Death of Chatham," and other much engraved pictures, and his son, who became Lord Chancellor Lyndhurst, and who died here in 1863.

At No. 3, Madame de Stael stayed when on her visit to this country, and here probably posed as untiringly as we know she did at Lansdowne House. Admiral Hawke once lived at No. 7, and next door, at No. 8, David Mallet, for whom is claimed, in common with James Thomson, the authorship of "Rule Britannia," which was first written as a lyric in that Masque which the joint authors produced for Frederick, Prince of Wales.

Besides Copley, two other artists once resided in George Street; Sir William Beechey and Sir Thomas Phillips; neither perhaps in the first flight, but both untiring wielders of the brush, and in their day successful portrait painters.

Richard Brinsley Sheridan's bright eyes and bardolphian face must often have lighted up the street as he listened to the chimes at midnight, at No. 9; and at an earlier day, the somewhat solemn visage of Lord Chancellor Cowper was to be seen here as he passed stately up the steps of No. 13, where his wife may have been penning that valuable diary which has come down to us. The list might be carried on interminably. Only one or two more names, and we must hurry into Hanover Square. The Earl of Albemarle and Lord Stair, of George II.'s day, lived in this street; and in 1762, the witty Lady Mary Wortley Montagu, who once, on someone's hinting that her hands were in need of ablution, replied, "You should see my feet," and whom Walpole described ungallantly as "always a dirty little thing." Who else can I pick out? Sir Charles Clarges, in 1726; Colonel Francis Charteris, three years later, and Lord Shelburne, in 1748. These, and how many others, pass by like ghosts and carry us back to "the snows of yesteryear!"

HANOVER SQUARE.

As we look up George Street, the pleasant green oasis of Hanover Square's central garden faces us, grouped round the great statue of Pitt which Chantry designed, and which was put up in 1831. There is no inscription on the base other than the name and dates of birth and death; but Sydney Smith, for once departing from his usual genial humour, wrote a suggested epitaph for it, so galling and so bitter, that it might have drawn the ghost of the "pilot that weathered the storm" from the shades where such great spirits dwell, and set it wandering with uneasy footsteps round its bronze counterfeit!

The Square was formed between the years 1716 and 1720. Being part of that great property which came to Harley, second Earl of Oxford, through his marriage, in 1713, with the Lady Henrietta Cavendish Holles, heiress of John, Duke of Newcastle. It was at first intended to call it Oxford Square, and only a loyal afterthought was responsible for its present designation. Notwithstanding that it has almost entirely lost that residential character with which it began its fashionable career, there luckily survive some of the original houses—Nos. 17 and 18 being cases in point—but the majority have been rebuilt out of all knowledge. To-day in these are found clubs, fashionable dressmakers, learned societies, anything you will but private residents; but in past times it held its own with any of the West End squares in the celebrity and importance of its inhabitants.

For instance, No. 13, known as Harewood House, which until recently was associated with the Royal Agricultural Society, was built by William Adam for the bibliophilic Duke of Roxburgh. Its present name was given it when the Earl of Harewood purchased it in 1795, and it remained in his family for just upon a century. At what was formerly numbered 15, but now 17, lived Mrs. Jordan, the beautiful and talented actress who fascinated the Duke of Clarence, afterwards William IV. Angelica Kauffmann was employed to decorate the principal ceiling here, and marbles from Italy were used in the formation of the beautiful mantelpieces. Next door (now

No. 18), where, in 1824, Sir John Malcolm inaugurated the Oriental Club, was, from 1771, for ten years occupied by Lord Le Despenser, who, as Sir Francis Dashwood, was one of the most notorious of that band of Medmenham monks, whose "Hell Fire Club," with its orgies, in which John Wilkes was one of the protagonists, was the scandal of the day. When the Oriental Club was formed the house was rebuilt, in 1827, by the Wyatts, for its accommodation.

Another important house in the Square was Downshire House, built in 1793, and once the residence of Lord Hillsborough. To-day it is a Bank; but in 1835 Prince Talleyrand was living here, and its walls may have heard some of the brilliant "*mots*" which this extraordinary man was wont to enunciate in what Sydney Smith described as "gurgling, not talking." Yet another celebrated individual is associated with the place, for, after Talleyrand's departure, Earl Grey, the hero of the great Reform Bill, lived here for a time. Two doors off once resided Lord Palmerston; not the "Pam" of the satirists and whilom Prime Minister, but his father; while later the Duchess of Brunswick, sister of George III., died in the same house in 1813.

If we can call "Lansdowne the polite," as Pope terms him, a poet, and Ambrose Phillips one (he does to some extent deserve the title), then Hanover Square has been the home of the muses; and indeed, since I can add the name of Thomas Campbell, there should be no doubt about the matter, for all three lived, and two of them died here; the first in 1735, the second fourteen years later. The United Services have also contributed their share of inhabitants, and great ones at that, for not only Field-Marshal Lord Cobham, to whom Pope dedicated his "Characters of Men," but also Lord Rodney, (who was the first to make use of that manœuvre of "breaking the line," which Nelson carried into such deadly effect at Trafalgar), and Lord Anson, a hardly less brilliant naval commander, all resided in the precincts of the Square.

Perceval Pott is hardly remembered to-day, but in his time he was a great surgeon; Sir James Clark, physician to the late Queen Victoria, is better known, and as both these benefactors to the ills of humanity lived in the Square, medicine may be said to have been well represented here in the past. Let me make an end of names with that of Mr. Hamilton, whose "single speech," so full of promise, is invariably associated with him, and who once occupied a house here.

It was in Hanover Square that the fine building erected by Sir John Gallini in 1771, was opened as the Hanover Square Concert Rooms, where John Christian Bach gave for eight years a series of concerts, and where later the "Ancient Music Society," and later still, the Philharmonic Society, drew crowded audiences, and may be regarded as the first serious and successful attempts to make classical music popular in this country. In 1862 the rooms were enlarged and redecorated, and, as the "Queen's Concert Rooms" held on gallantly for thirteen years, when they went the way of all musical flesh in London!

Let us now return and cross Bond Street, and, casting an eye up South Molton Street, where a stone on No. 36 indicates that the thoroughfare was formed in 1721; and not forgetting that the painter-poet and extraordinary visionary William Blake was living there, at No. 17, in 1807, let us wander up Brook Street.

BROOK STREET.

With Brook Street we enter into the purlieus of Mayfair, which stands for the West End, as Whitechapel does for the East, in those points of social habit characteristic of the two extreme quarters of the town.

Like so many of the thoroughfares in this quarter of London, Brook Street has gone through its second and third baptism, for first it was called Little Brook Street, and later Lower Brook Street. The stream once known as the Tyburn, which followed in its course South Molton Lane, across Brook Street, through the gardens of Lansdowne House to Buckingham Palace, is responsible for the name of Brook Street, but the pedestrian will need to pass over no bridges now on his way to Pimlico.

Statesmen and doctors, musicians and painters, have all in the past helped to give an interest to Brook Street, which to-day must chiefly rely on its fashionable residents, with here and there a stray politician, for what of interest it may be said to possess. It is still undoubtedly a fine street, and not a few of its houses help to carry us back to past days. Once Edmund Burke lived in it, at what is now No. 72. The great Handel's spinet may have been heard through the open windows of No. 57 as he tried, shall we say, the exquisite air from "Rinaldo," or gave the finishing touches to that "Water music" which was to charm (if his ears ever could be charmed by sweet sounds) his gracious Majesty King George II. We had better not intrude too curiously into the workshop of genius, or we might receive a shock, if we found its master not intent on some inspired number from the "Messiah," but spoiling one of his few books (a presentation copy, perchance, and oh! the feelings of the author), with fingers greasy with muffins, or indulging in one of his gargantuan feasts at which he alone was "de gompany." It would be like coming upon the great Beethoven, not in the throes of the Ninth Symphony, or the "Waldstein"; but hurling cups and saucers at his terrified maidservant!

Not far from Handel's lodgings (on the wall of which, by the bye, a tablet reposes) a painter, and an engraver plied their quieter arts and laboured in their "unregarded hours," for here both Gerard Vandergucht and his artist son Benjamin lived, and here were finished, with infinite pains, those engravings in which the elder man reproduced the refinement of Vandyck and the strength of Dobson. Thomas Barker (Barker of Bath, as he is termed) also painted in Brook Street; and the healing-art has been represented here by such medical names to conjure disease with as Jenner and Gull, Williams, Savory, and Broadbent. Sir Charles Bell, who died here in 1832, and Lord Davey, who happily is still with us, represent science; and Lord Lake, one of the famous of those, who, as Carlyle put it, "get their living by being killed"—the art of war.

Dear old Mrs. Delany, who was always young, and yet makes us think of her as always old and charming, lived here; and Sydney Smith, with whom we are for ever meeting (never too often, however), cut his jokes, (in which was often hidden so much genial philosophy), in Brook Street, among innumerable other places in London; while readers of "Dombey and Son" will remember that Cousin Feenix's "dull and dreary" residence was in this fashionable thoroughfare. Claridge's Hotel is in Brook Street, as most people know; but it looks very different to-day to what it must have done when the father of "Little Dorrit" stayed there on his return from the Continent.

GROSVENOR STREET.

By taking a short cut down Avery Row we shall find ourselves in Grosvenor Street, which was formed about 1726, and was a later addition to that great building development which was begun by Sir Richard Grosvenor in 1695. In size and appearance it is analogous to Brook Street. If Lord Balcarres lives in the former, have we not Earl Carrington in the latter? If Brook Street can boast Lord Davey, cannot Grosvenor Street glory in the presence of Queen Victoria's trusted physician, Sir James Reid; and till recently the Right Hon. James Lowther, Speaker of the House of Commons, and officially first of the untitled ones of England? And in the past a similar comparison could be sustained. We have noted some of the interesting residents of a bygone day in Brook Street; let us glance for a moment at those who once lived here. We can begin with a Prime Minister; for Lord North, that amiable and somnolent first Minister of the Crown, whose equanimity allowed him to peacefully doze while the Opposition was successfully voting the overthrow of his Government, lived here, in 1740; in the same year Sir Paul Methuen, the ancestor of Lord Methuen, the distinguished soldier of our own day, was residing here. Then there is that Miss Lane, notorious if for nothing else, at least for being the mistress of Frederick, Prince of Wales—the "Fritz" of many a popular, and generally scurrilous, ballad.

A later period brings before us the figure of Lord Crewe; and the Marquis Cornwallis, who was living in Grosvenor Street for five years (1793-8) before he went to reside in Grafton Street; and William Huskisson, whose tragic death saddened the inauguration of the first railway line in England. Samuel Whitehead was another old Parliamentary hand who was living here in 1800, as was Sir Humphrey Davy (at No. 28) eighteen years later, and before he removed to his last residence in Park Street, on the other side of the Square; and still later, that fashionable physician of the day, Matthew Baillie, whose merits, Moore, and Rogers (who once said that "bile and Baillie were his only companions") were never tired of advertising.

BRUTON STREET.

As we return southwards again, by way of Bond Street, we come to Bruton Street, which faces Conduit Street, but was not formed till nearly fifteen years after that thoroughfare.

As in most of the streets in this quarter there are several fine old houses to be found here, two of them, Nos. 17 and 22, being particularly noticeable. Here the great Duke of Argyle and Greenwich drew his last breath, in 1743. Six years later Horace Walpole came from Bolton Row to live here, many years before he succeeded to that title which he affected to consider such a weariness to the flesh.

But a greater than Walpole makes Bruton Street memorable, for here, in the year in which George III. ascended the throne, was residing William Pitt; so, too, some quarter of a century later, was Sheridan before he went to one of many subsequent residences in George Street, Whitehorse Street, Queen Street, and Savile Row.

Indeed Bruton Street seems always to have been a favourite resort of statesmen, and among lesser lights of the political world—and few will find fault at being placed among the smaller constellations by the side of such planets as Sheridan and Pitt—we find living here at various times Lord Hobhouse, Lord Granville, Lord Chancellor Cottenham, and, perhaps another planet, George Canning, in 1809, after he had left Maddox Street. Painting has been represented by William Owen, R.A., who died here in 1825; and medicine, by Sir Matthew Tierney, who was a resident in 1841.

GRAFTON STREET.

As we approach the Piccadilly end of Bond Street, only one more turning intervenes before we stand again at Stewart's Corner; this is the small Grafton Street, forming as it were a boundary to both Albemarle and

Dover Streets, which run into it. It takes its name from that Duke of Grafton who lived in the family mansion at the corner of Clarges Street, and who was associated with Lord Grantham in 1735, in the purchase of the property through which it runs.

Not always has it borne even the title of a street, for once it was known as "Ducking Pond Row," which would seem to indicate the vicinity of fields and one of those pieces of water in which recalcitrant spouses, when the "scold's bridle" failed in effect, were solemnly placed in a "ducking stool," and lowered into watery depths until their powers of "nagging" were deemed to have been thoroughly eradicated.

At a still later date, 1767 to wit, Grafton Street was known as "Evans Row," but its more euphonious title has long since been restored to it. London knows it chiefly on account of the Grafton Galleries which are situated at No. 7, and which annually attract crowds of art lovers. The celebrated Dilettanti Society and their fine collection of portraits are now housed here. Several clubs, notably the Turf, the Green Park Club, and the New Club, have their headquarters in Grafton Street, the latter club in the house, No. 4, in which Lord Brougham lived and died in 1848, after he had left Berkeley Square.

Another great statesman also once resided in Grafton Street, in the person of Charles James Fox, who was here, in 1783, before he moved to his temporary lodging at an hotel in Berkeley Square, and afterwards to the house in which we have met him in Clarges Street. When Mrs. Fitzherbert left Upper Grosvenor Street she came to live in Grafton Street in 1796; and among other notable inhabitants of the past, the names of Admiral Earl Howe, who died here, at No. 11, in 1799; Lord Stowell, at No. 16; the Marquis Cornwallis, subsequently to his sojourn in Grosvenor-Street; and the Right Honourable George Tierney, in 1809, occur to me.

HAY HILL.

If we leave Grafton Street, where it turns at right angles and continues without break into Dover Street, we shall see on our right a sharp declivity leading into Berkeley Square; this is Hay Hill, named from a farm which once stood here—if one can possibly imagine anything of the sort in this locality, unless the trees in Lansdowne House gardens, which are seen at the bottom of the hill, are sufficient to carry our minds to anything so rural. The Tyburn flowed at the foot of Hay Hill, as we have seen, and perhaps a water mill creaked noisily where nowadays the hoofs of toiling horses grind the pavement. In any case it seems to have been a desirable possession, for I find that, in 1617, it was granted to Hector Johnstone, who afforded help, probably of a monetary character, to that unfortunate Elector Palatine of

Bohemia, whose father-in-law, our own pacific James I., was so dilatory in assisting.

At a later date, in Queen Anne's day to wit, it was granted to the Speaker of the House of Commons, who eventually sold it, and gave the £200 which he thus obtained for it to the poor. If proof were wanted of the sudden and immense increase in the value of property in the West End, we have it in the fact that, before 1759, the same estate was disposed of by the Pomfret family, into whose possession it had come, for the very respectable sum of £20,000 odd.

Hay Hill has its historical importance, for here the heads of Sir Thomas Wyatt and three of his adherents were exposed after the failure of the well-known attempt to unthrone Queen Mary in 1554; and here George, Prince of Wales, with the Duke of York, returning from one of their frequent nightly revels, was held up by a highwayman, and the combined resources of the heir to the throne and his brother amounted to just half a crown!

BERKELEY SQUARE.

At the bottom of Hay Hill, we are in Berkeley Square, in many respects the most interesting of London's "quadrates," as they were once termed. It was formed on portions of the grounds of Berkeley House, and Evelyn, the Diarist, helped to lay out the estate, of which it is a part. Lansdowne House, with its gardens, occupies the south side of the square. This magnificent example of Adam's work was erected for Lord Bute, George III.'s unpopular Minister, but was sold by him, in a yet unfinished state, to the Earl of Shelburne, the ancestor of the Marquis of Lansdowne, who now occupies it. It naturally dwarfs all the other houses in the square, but many of these are also full of interest.

At No. 6 lived the second Lord Chatham, and here William Pitt sometimes stayed; close by, at No. 10, Sir Colin Campbell lived and died; and next door to his residence was the last of Horace Walpole's homes in London, now indicated by a tablet.

Other interesting people whose names have in the past been connected with Berkeley Square include Colley Cibber, and Charles James Fox; Lord Clive, who committed suicide at No. 45, and Lord Brougham, who occupied in turn two houses here; Lord and Lady Clermont, in whose house the beautiful Duchess of Devonshire took refuge from the Gordon Rioters, and Lady Anne Lindsay, who wrote "Auld Robin Gray"; Lord Canterbury, once Speaker of the House of Commons when Mr. Manners Sutton; and Child, the banker, whose daughter ran away with Lord Westmorland, and whose house, No. 38, now rebuilt, is the residence of the Earl of Rosebery. In fact the whole square is full of memories, social, historical, and political, and clinging about almost every house are recollections of the witty, the powerful, and the illustrious, who have at one time or another dwelt within their walls.

From Berkeley Square and its adjacent streets we enter into that large district known as Mayfair, which in the next chapter we shall have all our work cut out to even superficially examine.

THE MAY FAIR IN 1716.

CHAPTER V.

MAYFAIR.

*"Gay mansions with supper-rooms and dancing-rooms—
full of light and music."*—CARLYLE, "SARTOR RESARTUS."

Compared with London as a whole, Mayfair is quite a small quarter; but regarded as a congeries of innumerable streets, and two large squares, it is an extensive and intricate area, and a summer's day might well be exhausted before we had investigated all the twists and turns of its maze-like complexity.

It is true that its northern half has some sort of method due to Sir Richard Grosvenor's development of the great Westminster property, of which Grosvenor Square is the key-note; but its southern portion is, with here and there an exception, wanting in logical form, and threatens, I fear, to make the perambulation of it somewhat confusing to those to whom London is a sort of *terra incognita*.

It will be well to take Grosvenor Square as our starting-point, but before we set out a word must be said about the name, which is generic to the whole area. It almost speaks for itself; and is derived from that "Fair" formerly held here during the first fortnight in May, and dating from the time of James II. Unlike our conception of fairs, however, this one was instituted specifically "for musick, showes, drinking, gaming, raffling, lotteries, stage-plays, and drolls," and appears to have had nothing to do with the traffic and barter with which we are accustomed to associate these fast disappearing institutions. Nor was it merely the resort of the *profanum vulgus*; the nobility and gentry, we are told, made a point of frequenting it; and the fields in which it was held,—for then all this part was occupied by meadows and open ground—must have presented a gay appearance, with its booths and shows, surrounded by a brilliantly dressed throng, brought into still greater prominence by the more soberly attired crowd which surrounded it.

The "May Fair" continued as a regular institution until 1708, when it was put a stop to, chiefly on account of the disorders arising from it, and the questionable company that attended its equally questionable exhibitions; but partly on account, no doubt, of the erection of houses and the formation of streets, which began about this time. It, however, died hard, and was intermittently revived, in gradually lessening form; prize-fighting, boxing, and bull-baiting taking the place of "stage-plays and musick," till nearly the end of the 18th century, when it ceased altogether to exist, and left only its name as evidence of its former vitality.

DAVIES STREET.

Before entering Grosvenor Square, Davies Street has a particular interest in that it takes its name from that Mary Davies, daughter of Alexander Davies, of Ebury, who married Sir Thomas Grosvenor, and through whom the bulk of this great property came into the possession of the Westminster family.

At its Oxford Street end, Davies Street practically forms one with South Molton Lane, which at the beginning of the 18th century rejoiced in the not very euphonious designation of Shug Lane. There is, however, little to delay us here, unless we have a mind to glance into the modern church of St. Anselm, designed by Messrs. Balfour and Thackeray Turner, in the Byzantine style, and opened about eleven years since. I may, however, remind the reader that "Joe" Manton, the great gunmaker, carried on business at Nos. 24 and 25; and also that Tom Moore was living in the street, in 1817.

Turning into Brook Street, let us enter Grosvenor Square at its north-east corner.

GROSVENOR SQUARE.

Grosvenor Square is the largest (it is about six acres in extent) and, in some respects, the most fashionable of London's "quadrates." It was formed in 1695, by that great builder Sir Richard Grosvenor, who employed Kent, the celebrated landscape gardener, to lay out the central enclosure, in which once stood the statue of George I. by Van Nost. It was on this spot that the citizens of London, when setting up those defences against the Royalists, in 1642, on which we found them engaged when we were wandering in the Green Park, erected an earthwork, known as Oliver's Mound, from which we may probably infer the personal superintendence of the future Protector, or at least his rapidly growing influence.

As to-day nearly every house in Grosvenor Square is occupied by some influential or notable individual, so in the past has, practically, each been the home of an interesting personality. The great Earl of Chesterfield was living here in 1733, until he moved to the new mansion he had erected for himself facing the Park, and here it was that Johnson was "repulsed from his doors" or "waited in his outward rooms." Chesterfield, it will be remembered, married the daughter (she was then termed the niece) of that ill-favoured mistress of George I., Melusina de Schulemberg, created by her royal admirer, Duchess of Kendal, who, by the bye, also resided in the Square. The Marquis of Rockingham, once for a short time Prime Minister, died here in 1782, and Lord North, another Prime Minister, just ten years later, after he had left his former residence in Grosvenor Street, where we have already met with him.

Besides these two first ministers of the Crown, politics have been represented by a number of other well-known names, from which I can but pick out those of Lord Chancellor Hardwicke, who was here for half a dozen years; the Earl of Harrowby, at whose house—formerly No. 39, but now 44—the Cato Street conspirators hoped to make a holocaust of the entire Government; Lord Canning, in 1841, and another member of the same gifted family, Lord Stratford de Redclyffe, who died here in 1880, and whose effigy may be seen beside that of Lord Canning in the Abbey. Thomas Raikes, who was called by the wits "Phœbus Apollo," because he rose in the east and set in the west—an allusion to his dual connection with the City and Mayfair—was one of Grosvenor Square's past inhabitants of interest. Raikes is now remembered by his diary, a valuable record of his times, and his correspondence and friendship with Wellington, but his brother Robert, the initiator of Sunday Schools, carved out a name, *aere perennius*, for himself, and by its reflected light Thomas is also partially illuminated. That curious compound of genius and eccentricity, William Beckford, who wrote "Vathek" in three days and nights without intermission, and, what is more, wrote it in French, also lived here, at No. 22. Here was housed a portion of that extraordinary collection of pictures, books, furniture, and bric-a-brac which came, through the marriage of Miss Beckford with the Duke of Hamilton, into the possession of the latter; and the dispersal of which, in the eighties, was the sensation of the season, and crowded Christie's and Sotheby's with a wondering and envying throng.

Beckford used to be visited here by Lord Nelson and Lady Hamilton, two of the very few people he would ever admit to view the wonders of Fonthill, his Wiltshire seat, from the doors of which fairy palace he once repulsed George IV. himself. *Apropos* there is a story of a man forcing his way into Fonthill by some subterfuge, and being entertained *en grand seigneur* by the owner. When, however, the hour for retiring came, Beckford led him to the front door, and wished him good-night, adding that he had better *be careful of the bloodhounds*. The wretched man then realised that he was alone in a vast Park with no companions but his host's formidable guardians, and he is said to have passed the night in the first tree he could climb.

A story is a story, but this one has carried us many a mile from Grosvenor Square. One connected with the Square itself, however, tells how Dr.

Johnson once knocked down a sturdy beggar in its precincts, what time probably the great Cham of literature was on his way to visit his friends, the Thrales, who lived here for a time, until the death of Henry Thrale, in 1781. The town house of the Stanley family was in this Square till 1832, when they removed to St. James's Square, and here Lord Derby married Miss Farren, in 1797, in the same year in which John Wilkes, who was then residing at No. 30 (now No. 35), died. Sir Stamford Raffles, Lord Granville, Lord Shaftesbury, the philanthropist, and Sir John Beaumont, are among the many other notable people who have helped to shed lustre upon Grosvenor Square. The Square has been twice renumbered, with the exception of the east side, where the owners made such successful efforts to preserve the original numbering that even parochial authority gave way before them. Once, at an earlier day, the inhabitants made an equally strenuous but less defensible attempt to contest innovation; and it was not till 1842, *credite posteri*, that the Square was lighted with gas, it being the last important place in London to be so illuminated.

NORTH AND SOUTH AUDLEY STREETS.

At the north-west corner of the Square is North Audley Street, taking its name from Hugh Audley, while its continuation at the south-west, where it finally debouches into Curzon Street, is known as South Audley Street. Its most important mansion, one of the most beautiful in London, is Chesterfield House, facing Hyde Park through Stanhope Street. It was built by the great Earl of Chesterfield in 1749, Ware being the architect. Although it still preserves its fine courtyard, its fair proportions at the back, where its gardens formerly extended down the better part of Curzon Street, have been greatly curtailed by the erection of houses. The mansion itself, however, with its wonderful drawing-room, its library, where Lord Chesterfield lounged or wrote his celebrated "Letters to his Son," which Johnson criticised so pithily and so severely—its marble staircase and Ionic portico, both of which came from Canons, and gave the Earl the opportunity for a mild jest about his "canonical pillars," still remain. In 1869, Mr. Magniac gave the enormous sum of £175,000 for the place, and here housed his wonderful collections; but these have gone the way (Christie's way) of all beautiful things, and to-day Lord Burton owns the place.

But Chesterfield House is not the only fine mansion in Audley Street, for, at No. 8, is Alington House, now Lord Alington's, but formerly known as Cambridge House, where, in 1826, the Duke of York, brother of George IV. was living.

In another mansion, formerly called Bute House, once lived during the earlier years of George III.'s reign, and died in 1792, that Earl of Bute whose unpopularity I have before mentioned, and whose intimate friendship with the Princess Dowager of Wales (the widow of "Fritz," and mother of George III.) gave rise to so many ill-natured and probably quite erroneous reports. Home, who wrote the now forgotten tragedy of "Douglas," and who was a close friend of Lord Bute, was living in South Audley Street at the same time. Home was naturally a gifted man, but was also one of those who experienced the unhappy fate of being over-eulogized by an uncritical generation, and Shakespeare's fame was deemed to totter before his work. What he is now probably best remembered by is the famous reply of Dr. Johnson, to whom one of Home's admirers quoted with enthusiasm his line: "Who rules o'er freemen should himself be free." "Why, sir," replied Johnson, "one might as well say: 'Who kills fat oxen, should himself be fat!'"

Close to St. Mark's church in North Audley Street, lived, at various times, quite a bevy of notable ladies. Maria Edgeworth was one of these, and Lady Suffolk another, and Mary and Agnes Berry, before they went to reside in Curzon Street, where we shall presently meet with them.

All sorts and conditions of interesting people have resided in South Audley Street. Regardless of chronology, let me set down some of their names at random, commencing appropriately with a great church dignitary, Archbishop Markham, who died here in 1807; then, there was General Paoli, the Corsican patriot; Sir William Jones, famous for his learning, and Westmacott for his perpetuation in stone of many a learned one; Lord John Russell, Prime Minister, reformer, author, what you will; and Holcroft, whose name as a dramatist is forgotten for ever; Queen Caroline, that injudicious but badly used woman, who, on her arrival from Italy in 1820, stayed at the house of Wood, who championed her cause; Baron Bunsen, the clear-sighted diplomatist, and Louis XVIII., that gastronomic monarch, and his brother, Charles X., who, under the evil guidance of Prince Polignac, lost a throne that had cost so many lives and so much money to recover.

PARK STREET.

Park Street runs parallel with Audley Street. Formerly known as Hyde Park Street, it was one of the later developments of this part of the town, although it was formed anterior to 1768, in which year the actress Nelly O'Brien is stated to have died in it. A very different person also lived here (in No. 113) at a later day, in the person of that Lydia White, who, till the end of her life, delighted to gather around her the lions of the day. One of the last of these to visit her was Scott, who records in his diary that, on November 13th, 1826, he "found her extended on a couch, frightfully swelled, unable to stir, rouged, jesting, and dying." Harness, writing to

Dyce, at an earlier period, tells an anecdote illustrating her readiness of repartee:—"At one of Miss Lydia White's small and most agreeable dinners in Park Street, the company (most of them, except the hostess, being Whigs) were discussing in rather a querulous strain the desperate prospects of their party. 'Yes,' said Sydney Smith, 'we are in a most deplorable condition; we must do something to help ourselves; I think we had better sacrifice a Tory virgin.' This was pointedly addressed to Lydia White, who, at once catching and applying the allusion to Iphigenia, answered, 'I believe there is nothing the Whigs would not do to raise the wind.'" This "really clever creature," as Sir Walter calls her, died at her house here in 1827. Sir Humphrey Davy also came to live here, from Grosvenor Street, in 1825, and remained a resident till his death, two years after that of Miss Lydia; and Richard Ford, who made a guide-book to Spain, a permanent work of literary charm, was another of the street's past notable inhabitants.

GREEN STREET.

A few steps southward will bring us to Green Street, in which stands Hampden House, now the residence of the Duke of Abercorn.

No. 56 Green Street was formerly known as the "bow-window house," and here Miss Farren, who afterwards became Countess of Derby, once resided, and gave those suppers to "all the pleasantest people in London," which Hume, Walpole, and Lord Berwick have recorded. Sydney Smith died in Green Street, at Miss Farren's old house, in 1845, and here it was that he once told his doctor that he felt so feeble that if anyone were to put a pin into his hand he would not have strength enough to stick it into a Dissenter!

NORFOLK STREET.

Between Green Street and Park Lane intervenes the little Norfolk Street, at a house in which Lord William Russell was barbarously done to death by his valet in 1840. Here Lady Hesketh, the friend of Cowper; Sir James Mackintosh; and, later, Lord Overstone, the millionaire banker, resided.

UPPER BROOK STREET.

A little further on is Upper Brook Street, where once lived Lord George Gordon, famous for his connection with the anti-Catholic riots, which, had not George III. acted with splendid promptitude, might have resulted in a holocaust of London. Here also resided George Grenville, the statesman and creator of that marvellous library which is, to-day, one of the wonders of the British Museum; Mrs. Damer, the talented friend of Horace Walpole, for whom she executed the Eagle which once stood in the Tribune at Strawberry Hill; and Hamilton, of "single speech" fame.

UPPER GROSVENOR STREET.

As Upper Brook Street joins the north side of Grosvenor Square with Park Lane, so Upper Grosvenor Street leads directly from its southern side to that latter-day synonym for worldly riches.

Here lived such notable people as Lord Erskine, the great lawyer, Sir Robert Peel, and also Lord Crewe, who appears to have moved hither from Grosvenor Street, or, as we ought to say, Lower Grosvenor Street. But the chief feature of the street is Grosvenor House, the well-known residence of the Duke of Westminster, the fine screen and gates of which, designed by Candy, were put up in 1842, and form a curious break in the otherwise unbroken regularity of the houses. I shall have something to say about Grosvenor House, when we come to Park Lane; so that now we need not interrupt our walk, which in a moment will bring us to Mount Street, taking its name from "Oliver's Mound," formerly in Grosvenor Square.

MOUNT STREET.

Mount Street dates from about 1740, but since then it has been wholly rebuilt with red-brick structures, the majority of which are now shops, with flats above them, and thus preserves nothing of its earlier character, when such as Lady Mary Coke, the compiler of a most valuable and delightful diary, Fanny Burney (Madame D'Arblay), whose work in the same direction is, known to all the world, and Sir Henry Holland, who has also left us his reminiscences, lived in it.

From Mount Street we pass easily, by way of South Audley Street, to that congeries of thoroughfares, which lie between Berkeley Square and Park Lane.

ALDFORD STREET.

If we take those on the east, we shall first come to Aldford Street, which was known for a century and a half (until 1886) as Chapel Street. Much of the street has been rebuilt, and therefore some of its intrinsic interest has disappeared, notably the house in which Beau Brummell once lived, and where he was wont to receive the Prince Regent at those "*petits soupers*," and at those wonderful ceremonies of the toilet, the details of which Captain Jesse has recorded with so much gusto. But a greater than Brummell was once a resident in Aldford Street, for, at No. 23, the poet Shelley was staying in the same year (1813) in which we have encountered him in Half Moon Street. Beyond this solitary celebrity, however, there is nothing to delay our passing on to South Street, which runs parallel to Aldford Street in a southerly direction.

SOUTH STREET.

This street was formed about 1737, and till nearly the middle of the 18th century, the chapel attached to the Portuguese Embassy (formerly at 74, South Audley Street), where Garrick was married, was situated in it.

Brummell once lived here (at No. 24), and so did, in 1837, Lord Melbourne (at No. 39), while among other names of note connected with it mention may be made of Charles James Fox, Lord and Lady Holland, and John Allen, so indissolubly connected with the annals of Holland House; Mademoiselle d'Este, the daughter of the Duke of Sussex; the Duke of Orleans, better known as Philippe Egalité, and Miss Florence Nightingale whose name is a household word in two hemispheres.

DEANERY AND TILNEY STREETS.

Deanery Street passes by the side of Dorchester House (which I must leave for notice till we reach Park Lane) to Tilney Street. The former, a small serpentining thoroughfare, takes its name from the Dean and Chapter of Westminster, who are the ground-landlords, and to whom Lord Chesterfield made an amusing reference in his will. It was first called "Dean and Chapter Street," and was formed at the same time as South Street.

Tilney Street is perhaps chiefly remembered as the residence of Mrs. Fitzherbert, whose house was at the corner facing Park Lane, the bow windows of which still indicate it. Here it was that, in June, 1800, after their temporary separation, Mrs. Fitzherbert and her husband, George, Prince of Wales, were openly reconciled at a public breakfast, which "proclaimed to the fashionable world of London that her relations with the Prince were resumed on the old footing."

Soame Jenyns also lived in Tilney Street, and died there in 1787. Forgotten nowadays, he was in his time a prolific writer, and his style was considered as a model of clearness and ease. His epigram on Johnson is generally supposed to have been the only ill-natured thing he ever produced; here it is:—

"Here lies Sam Johnson. Reader, have a care;

Tread lightly, lest you wake a sleeping bear.

Religious, moral, generous, and humane

He was; but self-sufficient, proud and vain;

Fond of, and overbearing in, dispute;

A Christian and a scholar—but a brute!"

What would Miss Jenkins and Miss Pinkerton have said?

GREAT STANHOPE STREET.

At least two Prime Ministers have lived in Great Stanhope Street—Lord Palmerston, from 1814 to 1843, before he went to Piccadilly; and Sir Robert Peel, for five years from 1820; while Lord Brougham is given as residing at No. 4, in 1834, in occupancy of which house he had been preceded, respectively, by Lords Mansfield and Exeter.

To these may be added the names of two military veterans. Lord Raglan, in 1853, and Viscount Hardinge, who died at No. 15, three years later; as well as Colonel Barré, who lived at No. 12, where he died, in 1802.

Before proceeding into Curzon Street, let us return by way of South Audley Street, and turn into Waverton Street, which forms the west side of a species of gridiron of thoroughfares, of which Farm Street is the north side and Charles Street the south.

FARM STREET.

Farm Street is one of the thoroughfares that took their names from their association with those agricultural pursuits which we have nowadays such difficulty in associating with this fashionable neighbourhood. This "common pasturage" and the "milk maids" formerly connected with it, have been recently brought vividly to mind by the action of the "milk ladies" of St. James's Park, the lineal descendants of those of Mayfair, who successfully resisted an attempt to deprive them of their rights.

A Jesuit Church stands in Farm Street, that of the Immaculate Conception, which, it is interesting to remember, was the first regular church possessed by the Jesuits in London after their expulsion from Somerset House and St. James's under Charles I.

JOHN STREET.

John Street, laid out about 1730, running at right angles, connects Farm Street with Hill Street, and also possesses a church; in this case the well-known Berkeley Chapel, built about 1750, of which Sydney Smith and, later, Cary, the translator of Dante, were former incumbents. The chapel has been twice redecorated, in 1874 and 1895; and, apart from its associations, is worth a visit, if only to see the memorial window placed there to the memory of the late Duke of Clarence.

HILL STREET.

Hill Street, formed about 1742, probably takes its name from some inequality of the ground, more pronounced when all this part was fields than now when building development has been responsible for a generally levelling process.

Mrs. Montagu lived in Hill Street, while she was building for herself the fine mansion in Portman Square, where she covered the walls with birds' feathers and "wanton Cupids," and once a year entertained the chimney-sweeps of the district.

Another resident was that Admiral Byng, whose infamous execution called forth a well-known sarcasm from Voltaire; while others who lived here in the past were Lord Camden, the great Lord Chief Justice; Lord Brougham, before he received his title; the Earl of Malmesbury, whose four volumes of entertaining memoirs record his diplomatic experiences and successes at half the courts of Europe; and Lords Lyttelton and Carlisle, both poets of distinctly minor attainments. Other names might be added; but to be exhaustive would be to hamper the wings of imagination.

HAYES STREET.

Passing by Hayes Street, now used as mews by the exigencies of fashion, and where, at the corner, a public-house with its sign bearing the inscription, "I am the only running Footman," will recall to our minds this former appendage to fashionable state, of which "Old Q." was the last to make use, we come to Charles Street, thus named after Charles, Earl of Falmouth, a brother of Lord Berkeley, the ground-landlord.

CHARLES STREET.

This is the last of what I call "the gridiron," and is generally known as Charles Street, Berkeley Square, from its entering the square at its south-west corner.

Royalty in the person of William IV., when Duke of Clarence, has been represented in this street; while Sydney Smith, when he was incumbent of Berkeley Chapel close by, was residing here, at No. 33, the house in which the daughter of Lord Hervey was burnt to death, in 1815. It was about the purchase of this house that Smith once wrote "the lawyers discovered some flaw in the title about the time of the Norman Conquest, but, thinking the parties must have disappeared in the quarrels of York and Lancaster, I waived the objection!"

Among other residents I find the names of Lord Ellenborough, once Governor-General of India; Beau Brummell, at No. 42, in 1792; Lady Grenville, after the death of her husband, the Prime Minister; and Bulwer Lytton. The latter, in 1839, fitted up his house in a most lavish style, and one of the rooms was made to represent, as closely as might be, one of the chambers in Pompeii. James Smith, one of the authors of the "Rejected Addresses," has left an amusing account of a visit he once paid here.

CURZON STREET.

A few steps brings us into Curzon Street. It is curious to notice the difference between the two ends of this fashionable thoroughfare, or rather it was till the Duke of Marlborough set up his splendid mansion amidst the small shops and public-houses which distinguish the eastern part, where Bolton, Clarges, and Half Moon Streets dwindle away into it, and Lansdowne Passage forms an exiguous connection between it and Berkeley Street.

Once the street was known as Mayfair Row; its present designation being derived from the family name of Lord Howe, the owner of the property. If we except Sunderland House, the Duke of Marlborough's, (*apropos* of which the story is told that Queen Victoria once informed the Duke she had never been in Curzon Street, so prescribed are frequently the peregrinations of sovereigns) the chief mansion is Crewe House, the residence of the Earl of Crewe. Until comparatively recently it was known as Wharncliffe House, having been acquired by Mr. J. Stuart Wortley for £12,000, in 1818, and continuing in his family (later ennobled by the Barony of Wharncliffe) till its present owner bought it at a very different figure. Originally, in 1708, Mr. Edward Shepherd, who built Shepherd's Market opposite, in 1735, lived here; and, in 1750, it was purchased by Lord Carhampton for £500, if one can possibly believe in the adequacy of so small a sum to buy anything in such a neighbourhood!

So many illustrious people have lived and died in Curzon Street that pages might easily be filled with their names; but a few must here suffice, and appropriately, as living once at No. 1, since demolished, I find that great actress, Madame Vestris; and at No. 8, the celebrated Miss Berrys, who both died here in 1852, and lie buried in Petersham churchyard. Their house was once taken by Baron Bunsen, who records moving into it in 1841. Sir Henry Holford, the surgeon, who was one of those who gazed on the actual features of Charles I. when that monarch's coffin was opened, and who left an interesting account of the circumstance, died at a house in Curzon Street, in 1844; and at No. 19, Benjamin Disraeli, Earl of Beaconsfield, drew his last breath, in 1882.

Other residents whose names may be set down were Lord Marchmont, the friend of Pope; Mason, the poet; and Francis Chantry, the sculptor, long before he became famous; Lord Macartney, whose mission to China is to be found recorded in a bulky volume, and who, according to Walpole, occupied here a "charming house—cheap as old clothes," which once belonged to Lord Carteret.

Opposite Crewe House stands Curzon Chapel, or, as it is as often called, Mayfair Chapel. The original structure dated from 1730, but it was subsequently rebuilt, although it is so plain and ugly that it could not possibly have been improved by the process.

The chapel is notorious for those illegal marriages conducted by the Rev. Alexander Keith, until the scandal was put an end to here by his being unfrocked in 1742. But this action on the part of a justly incensed church did not deter him from carrying on the same practices at another chapel, which he inaugurated close by. What the Church was unable to do, the Law effected, and the subsequent passing of the Marriage Act, in 1754, finally put a stop to Mr. Keith's illicit activity. It is said that when told that the Bishops would stop his illegal marriages, he replied, "Let them; and I'll buy two or three acres of ground, and by God, I'll *under-bury* them all!"

Of those who took advantage of this short cut to wedlock were the Duke of Chandos, who was married (if the word can be permitted in such a connection) to Mrs. Anne Jeffrey, in 1744; Lord Strange and Lucy Smith, two years later; Lord Kensington and Rachel Hill, in 1749; and Lord George Bentinck and Mary Davies, in 1753.

The year before this last match, occurred the best-remembered of these "splicings," when the Duke of Hamilton was wedded at half-past twelve o'clock at night to the beautiful Elizabeth Gunning, who lived to be the wife of two and the mother of four dukes. Horace Walpole has left a vivid account of the ceremony, in which a ring torn from a curtain replaced that circlet of gold which is recognised as the more usual type of matrimonial bondage.

HERTFORD AND CHESTERFIELD STREETS.

Hertford Street, formed about 1764, now almost rivals Wimpole Street in the numbers of the medical profession who reside in it; but at an earlier day it was the home of politicians, with here and there a soldier, and here and there a poet; while it was in a house here that the Duke of Cumberland, brother of George III., was married to Mrs. Horton, in 1771.

Sheridan had one of his many residences here, at No. 10, in 1793, and Lord Charlemont, whose wife's name continues (in booksellers' catalogues) to be erroneously connected with a notorious translation of Voltaire's "Pucelle," was living in the street in 1766. So, too, were Lord Goderich, and the Earl of Mornington, some years later; and, in 1792, died here General Burgoyne, whose surrender to the American forces at Saratoga precipitated that independence which the United States soon after obtained.

The first Earl of Liverpool, father of the Prime Minister, died here in 1808; and Earl Grey was living in this street in 1799; while other politicians who have been former residents were Robert Dundas and Charles Bathurst, Lord Langdale and Bulwer Lytton, the last of whom lived at No. 36 from

1831 to 1834, and here wrote "Paul Clifford," "The Last Days of Pompeii," "Rienzi," "Alice," and "Ernest Maltravers." Lord Sandwich, the well-known "Jemmy Twitcher," died at No. 11, in 1792, and "Capability Brown," the great landscape gardener, at another house here, nine years earlier. But perhaps the street's chief claim to remembrance is the fact that Edward Jenner resided at No. 14, for some years, from about the beginning of 1803. Contrary to expectation, his fees fell off on his setting up here, and, together with the excessive rent he was obliged to pay, and the additional expenses of London life, he found it impossible to continue to reside here. A tablet now marks the house where this benefactor to the human race once fought his double fight against disease and poverty!

Chesterfield Street joins Chesterfield Gardens, which stand on the site of the once ample grounds of Chesterfield House. George Selwyn dates many of his letters from one of the houses in this street; while Beau Brummell was residing in another, No. 4, till 1810, and here he was visited often enough by the Prince of Wales, who sometimes remained so late that he was compelled, says Jesse, to insist on Brummell giving him a quiet dinner, which not uncommonly ended in a midnight debauch.

PARK LANE.

Park Lane stands alone among the streets of London. In that it has only one side, and looks directly into one of London's Parks, it might at first seem to have some analogy to the western end of Piccadilly; but Piccadilly is made up of clubs, with here and there a business establishment and—except at Hyde Park Corner itself—private houses but sparsely scattered down it; whereas Park Lane practically consists of the mansions of the wealthy. So much so is this the case, indeed, that it has latterly become synonymous with worldly riches, and is now the objective at which Socialistic and democratic stump orators level their sarcasms from their convenient vantage ground within the park railings; what time the law in helmet and white gloves smiles tolerantly, and the plutocrats lunch unmoved.

It will be well to start from its northern end, where it joins Oxford Street, or the Tyburn Road, as it was once called, for Park Lane used formerly to be known as Tyburn Lane, and close by the Marble Arch—permanently at rest after its journey from the front of Buckingham Palace—was Tyburn Tree, where the end of innumerable malefactors drew crowds of excited and unseemly witnesses.

It is somewhat anomalous that this "glass of fashion" among streets should have been, so comparatively recently as 1769, connected with such gruesome associations; but it is also equally difficult to imagine it as the dreary, unkept by-way which it was during the Augustan age, when millionaires were not; and the petrol of the motor was not smelt in the road.

GREAT HOUSES OF PARK LANE.

The first of the great mansions we come to is Brook House, which stands at the corner of Upper Brook Street. It was designed by Wyatt, and was for many years the residence of Lord Tweedmouth, and noted for the receptions held here, when the Liberal Party indulged in its revels.

A step and we come to Dudley House, built by the late Lord Dudley, and once the casket that contained many of those wonders of art which this most princely of peers loved to gather around him.

At the corner of Upper Grosvenor Street stands a sort of magnificent temple dedicated to music and the fine arts. This is the concert or ballroom which the late Duke of Westminster, apparently regardless of architectural symmetry, added to Grosvenor House, which is seen behind it. It reminds me of nothing so much as a beautiful pearl which has succeeded in emerging from the parent shell, but not wholly detaching itself from the parental ligaments.

As we have seen, the entrance to Grosvenor House is in Park Street; but I said nothing about the mansion then, because it seems to belong, as does its vast garden extending to Mount Street, to Park Lane. The residence, which was known as Gloucester House, at the time when the Duke of Gloucester, brother of George III., acquired it in 1761, is, of course, one of the great, as differentiated from merely large, houses of London, and it contains a collection of pictures and works of art which a millionaire would have to exhaust his fortune in purchasing, and which could only be adequately described by a Waagen or a Smith.

Just beyond South Street stands what I suppose few people, having regard to both its exterior and interior, will deny to be the finest private residence in London—Dorchester House, which was erected by Vulliamy, in the Italian Renaissance style, for the late Mr. Holford. Surrounded as it is by every conceivable kind of architectural experiment, it may be deemed out of place; but, taken by itself, it is a perfect reproduction on a lavish scale of those Italian palaces to which the blue sky of the South forms the one necessary background. The interior is commensurate, both in size and detail, with its commanding exterior, and only the pen of the late Mlle. de la Ramée ("Ouida") could do justice to the marble staircase. The art collection housed here is extraordinarily fine, while the yearly exhibitions of Old Masters at Burlington House are seldom without one or more examples from among the masterpieces which hang on the walls of Dorchester House.

It has frequently been let, sometimes as when the Shahzada was there, for a short period; sometimes, as now, when it has become the residence of the Hon. Whitelaw Reid, the United States Ambassador, for a term of years. Its perfection of taste and its rare and beautiful contents remind me that, appropriately enough, the Marquis of Hertford, whose name is indissolubly associated with such things, died here in 1842.

At the south corner of Stanhope Street we come to the last of the great houses of Park Lane—Londonderry House, now the residence of the Marquis of Londonderry, but formerly known as Holdernesse House, it having been erected by the Wyatts in 1850, on the site of the former town house of the Earls of Holdernesse.

Next door to Londonderry House is quite a small house of somewhat elaborate design. This was built on the site of another residence, by Mr. Whittaker Wright, whose name is remembered in connection with a notorious trial a few years since, and who, *"immemor sepulcri,"* as Horace says, built a house which he was never destined to enjoy, somewhat as in earlier days Baron Grant erected a palace in Kensington which was demolished before it was occupied.

At this point Park Lane splits itself into two thoroughfares, the smaller being Park Lane proper, and by its tenuity giving some *raison d'être* for its designation, the latter being known as Hamilton Place, which takes its name from that Hamilton who was Ranger of Hyde Park during the reign of Charles II., and who erected a number of small houses here in what was then but a *cul de sac*, on ground which formed an integral part of the park itself.

HAMILTON PLACE.

The houses in this street were rebuilt by Adam in 1809, but it was not till about sixty years later that the street was carried through to Park Lane, and became its chief outlet into Piccadilly.

The mansion (No. 1) at the corner of Piccadilly was built by Lord Chancellor Eldon when he left Bedford Square, and here he died in 1838. Next door was occupied, from 1810 to 1819, by the Duke of Bedford, who moved here from Great Stanhope Street; while later residents include Earl Gower, afterwards Duke of Sutherland, the Right Hon. Thomas Grenville, and the Duke of Argyll.

THE ENTRANCE TO PICCADILLY AT HYDE PARK CORNER, WITH ST. GEORGE'S HOSPITAL.

At No. 4, the great Duke of Wellington was living in 1814, while yet Apsley House was in the occupation of his brother, the Marquis Wellesley. Others who have lived here include the Earl of Lucan, in 1810, and Lord Grenville, twelve years later. In our own day it has been the town residence of the Earl of Northbrook, the head of the Baring family and some time Governor-General of India.

Mr. Leopold de Rothschild's beautiful house (No. 5), which looks directly on to the park and has a view up Park Lane, was, from 1810 to 1825, the residence of the Earl of Buckinghamshire, and many years later, of the Marquis Conyngham.

One of London's rare if not always beautiful statues stands at the junction of Park Lane and Hamilton Place. Utility has been combined with decoration in this case, for it also forms a fountain, presided over by the Muses of Tragedy, Comedy, and History—not Farce, as might have been expected, unless there be some subtly ironical meaning hidden in the otherwise illogical collocation. Above stand, in evident wonderment, Chaucer, Shakespeare, and Milton, in marble, and on the summit Fame puffs industriously at her trumpet. Thornycroft was responsible for this work, which was erected in 1875, at the cost of £5,000, the money being provided from the estate of an old lady who died intestate and without heirs.

Before we finally quit Park Lane one or two of its former interesting residents must receive a short word of notice. Thus, at the corner of Upper Grosvenor Street—at that time known as No. 1, Grosvenor Gate—Disraeli was living, from 1839 till 1873; and friend and brother novelist and politician, Sir Edward Bulwer Lytton, was residing in 1842 at what was known as No. 1 Park Lane, during which period "Zanoni" was published.

The names of Warren Hastings, Richard Sharp, and Lady Palmerston are also connected, *cum multis aliis*, with this famed street; and in one of those houses which look on to the Lane, but which have their entrances in other streets—in this case Seamore Place—lived the gorgeous Lady Blessington (1832-6), after her departure from St. James's Square and before her final apotheosis in Kensington Gore. The white-painted semi-circular front of her former residence at the corner of Pitt's Head Mews, may still be seen; and it will not take a great stretch of the imagination to picture that beautiful and talented woman surrounded by all that extravagance and luxury could suggest, sitting upon its balcony, and penning those short stories, or editing those wonderful "books of beauty," which formed the fashionable literary *pabulum* of early Victorian days.

Within a radius of half a mile from Stewart's corner of Old Bond Street we have traversed that part of the town which is associated pre-eminently with the fashionable, and in a lesser degree with the literary and artistic, traditions of two centuries of London life. Compared with the innumerable memories which its stones evoke, the area covered is a relatively small one, but had space here been less restricted, one might have gone on wandering over acres of paper while setting down the names of persons and places, and lingering over the stories and anecdotes with which they are connected.

FOOTNOTES:

[1] It has been suggested that the name may have had its origin in the famous "Pickadilla" cakes first made in old Pickadilla Hall, and made and sold at "Stewart's" to the present day. [Publisher's Note.]

[2] The great authority for it is Mr. Arthur Dasent's book, while I have a chapter on it in my "History of the Squares of London."—E. B. C.

[3] As an example of the rebuilding of Piccadilly, so rapidly going on during the last few years, a drawing of one of its handsomest structures, Denman House, at the corner of Air Street, is given. Built in 1903, it replaces the old building, where the late Mr. James L. Denman had been established for over half a century. Messrs. Denman & Co., having acquired the freeholds of the vineyards of the celebrated "J. Lemoine," Champagne, and also the "Chateau Livran" estate with its 350 acres of vines in the Medoc, required larger premises. Denman House was therefore built, from the designs of Mr. Harold A. Woodington, A.R.I.B.A. The upper part of the old building, which appears in the vignette, was

leased in the early fifties to the Marquis Townshend for the Pall Mall Club.—(Publishers' Note).

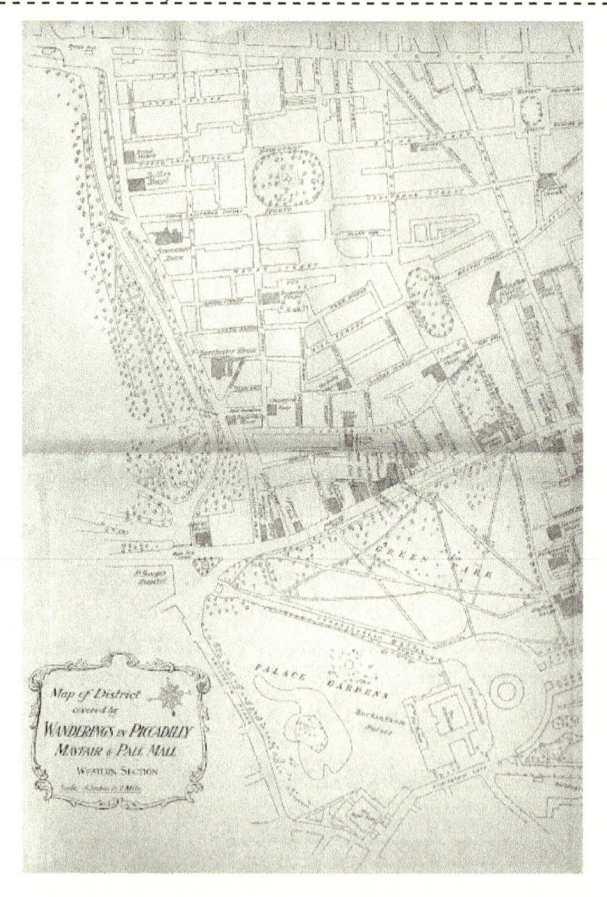

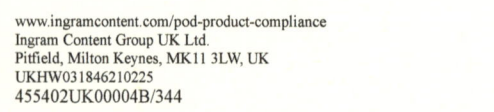